T0381102

All with God, Jesus and the Angels

Inspirational Stories from Psychic Medium

Bonnie Page

BALBOA.PRESS
A DIVISION OF HAY HOUSE

Balboa Press books may be ordered through booksellers or by contacting:

Balboa Press
A Division of Hay House
1663 Liberty Drive
Bloomington, IN 47403
www.balboapress.com
844-682-1282

Print information available on the last page.

ISBN: 979-8-7652-4891-1 (sc)
ISBN: 979-8-7652-4890-4 (e)

Library of Congress Control Number: 2024905439

Balboa Press rev. date: 04/16/2024

Dedication

I want to dedicate this book to my family and friends,
who always stick by me no matter what.

To My Husband, George

You have listened to stories about the spirit world since
we met 38 years ago, never doubting me for a moment
while always being my biggest supporter.

Following me from event to event, you play the role of my
bouncer and microphone guy and have never complained,
even though you hate to see the audience members cry.

Thank you for being a great husband, father, and soulmate, always
allowing me to be.

To My Son, Trevor

I know deep in my heart that you always have my back, and am so
blessed to have such a beautiful soul whose chose me to be his mom.
You are always a gift straight from God, and
thank you for making me a grammy.

To my brothers and sister

It sure is nice having siblings who love to talk about the spirit
world with me, and your support means everything.

To My Besties, Terry and Susan

If I didn't have you I don't know what I would do without your
friendship. Thank you for being a part of my journey and for
always listening to me and accepting me unconditionally. The

two of you are the sisters meant to be with me on this journey, and I appreciate you both. Here's to more fun and adventures!

And to all of my friends, clients and students

It's because of you that I am able to do the work that I love to do. Thank you for all of your continued support.

To ALL of You

THANK YOU!

God asked…I listened.

Hearing God's voice as he asked her to make mediumship her full-time profession, Bonnie asked him, 'Why?' And God replied, "The world is becoming darker and darker, and we need more light."

Listening to God's instructions, Bonnie opened her business, Messages from Heaven, and began sharing her gifts of seeing and hearing the spirit world. This proved that there is no death; our souls truly live on and are ever-present with the ones they love here.

With her popular weekly column and TV show called "Ask the Psychic Medium," Bonnie answers your questions about the afterlife, the spirit world, and how to navigate life here on earth. Bonnie's down-to-earth way of talking and writing makes her books easy to understand, sharing her love for the spirit world with you.

This book is a compilation of questions, answers, and real-life stories of growing up as a fourth-generation medium living in a small town, in a historical home filled with loving spirits, and always with God, Jesus, and the Angels.

Contents

Hearing the Voice of God

When I was a little girl, I would often hear a man's voice speaking to me, sometimes louder than other times. He seemed to know me well and was always there to comfort me. He would call me "little one".

Not knowing who this man's voice belonged to, I associated it with a loving grandfather who had passed when I was two. I thought it must be him trying to guide me. As I got older and still heard the voice, mostly when a big decision had to be made, this voice gave me a sense of knowing who was speaking to me.

One day, I asked who he was, and pleasantly enough, he gave me my answer. "Little one, it's God."

When God talks to me, I hear Him outside my head, and I know it's not my own or anyone else's thoughts. I feel He has led me this way with a plan all along of me doing the work I do and doing it with Him in mind. When I first started giving readings, I left Him out of the conversation as it was hard enough to come out of the closet by explaining that I could speak to the dead. (They are not that to me).

One day, driving down the road, there was that voice, "Little one, I need you not to separate me from your work." So, the next reading I gave I said my prayer out loud, as I always start a session with bringing in God, Jesus, and the angels. I feel totally surrounded by love as I ask your loved ones to talk to me.

I became more confident in my conviction of what I believe and have become more comfortable talking about my conversations with God. God always has a plan. We are just not always aware. I was a nail tech for many years and one day I asked God, "Why did you have me do nails so long?" He answered, "I was teaching you to counsel." Well, that was surely true, holding ladies' hands every day, listening to the stories of their lives, always trying to be a blessing, and wanting them to leave happier than when they came in. It seemed to make a difference.

Any time we are helping others, we are doing God's work. Prayers are heard!

When I was younger and in a nightclub (yes, God was there, too!), my now-husband asked me out on our first date. When I said yes, he held my chin in his fingers just like my dad always did (dad always being my hero), and when I turned around I heard, "You are going to marry him." Talk about predicting the future! I said, "What?"

Well, 36 years later we are still happily married. Thank you, God. He knows I listen.

Prayer is like having a conversation with God. I walk around talking to Him all the time and he hears. Please know that God wants to talk to all his children, and even if you are not hearing that voice, you might have a feeling, like when you hear people saying God has put something in my heart. Different people have different ways of having a relationship with God and the divine.

Recently, I was letting myself be worried about a situation, and I heard God's voice: "You are not having faith." I went to say, "Yes, I do," and then realized if I am worrying, I am not trusting that God knows best. Worrying will not get you where you want to go. Having faith might just do the trick.

I know we are human, and we can tend to get caught up in this earthly life, but if you look deep enough it's always a lesson that we need to learn. Do your best and follow the golden rule: Do unto others … and have faith.

Keep talking to God.

Angels Are All Around Us

Dear Bonnie: Do you ever see angels? I know you talk about them a lot, but do you actually see them like spirits? I would like to see them. So, if you could give me some tips on how to make them come to me, I would appreciate it. — Ruby.

Dear Ruby: Ever since I was a little girl, I had a fascination with God and the angels. I remember always feeling protected and I would stare at the picture my mom had in the house of an angel with the children around her.

As I got older, I would buy statues of the angels and would put them in every room in my house and outside in the garden.

I started reading countless books on angels and all the different kinds of angels and their strengths, but it wasn't until I started making my connection to the other side stronger that I opened myself up to actually seeing angels.

One night, I was reading a book about angels in bed, and I fell asleep with the book next to me. During the night, I became conscious of Archangel Michael sitting next to me, so close I could see him staring right back at me. I remembered to ask, "Who are you?" He responded, "I am Archangel Michael." On the other side of me was a much bigger-framed angel, and when I looked at him, he said, "I am Archangel Raphael. You are a healer like me."

Since that night, I have had several visits from Archangel Raphael, especially when I am giving a reiki session or need a healing for myself.

Archangel Michael is with me daily, and I hear him speak very easily and clearly.

Doing this work of mediumship and healing, I often need his help with his sword of love and light. I see him almost nightly, coming down and taking his sword and scooping the energy left on me by others.

When I first started to talk to Michael, I didn't let him stop having a conversation with me for two days. I asked him all sorts of questions — Why can I hear you so well? Why me? — all kinds of things until I finally asked, "Are you tired of talking to me?" He kindly answered, "No," and said he would be here whenever I needed him or to talk. He has, for sure, kept his word. When I give angel card readings or need advice for someone, he always answers.

I also have heard and seen many other angels, along with fairies, which are the elementals. They are the keepers of the flowers and nature, so if you like to work in your garden, call to them and ask for a sign. They are smaller and faster than other angels but very pretty and joyful.

One night, I awoke to a fairy coming toward me, and as she did, she came right up close and threw fairy dust at me!

Yup, you can't make this stuff up. I told her that was the nicest thing anyone had ever done for me.

Angels love it when you honor them by having statues or pictures of them. It makes them feel wanted. So, if you want an angel to visit you, start by learning as much about them as you can and invite them into your life.

They like to be asked, so remember to do so. It's like giving them permission to be with you.

They can step in and save you if it's a life-and-death situation without you asking.

I am sure you have heard the stories of people surviving death and not knowing how. It was likely the angels stepping in because it wasn't that person's time.

Angels are God's messengers and have never walked on Earth, so if you have a request, state it as simply as possible so they can respond.

The most important message I received came one night from two angels, twin brothers Sandalphon and Metatron.

These two angels that came to visit me during a meditation told me, "God wants you for something big." I said, "Okay," but forgot to ask what. That's okay. I am sure I'll find out.

There is a story of Elijah and Enoch, two twin brothers that did not die, and God took them to Heaven to be by his side, and they became Sandalphon and Metatron. Metatron is the name Enoch received after his transformation into an angel. Sandalphon is referred to as the prophet Elijah, transfigured and elevated to angelic status. I knew nothing about them until the day they visited me, and then I did my research.

Often when things happen in the spiritual world, I will do research so I might understand the full story behind them.

Angels Have Different Jobs

Dear Bonnie: I would like to get to know and feel the angels around me. Do you have a suggestion of where I should start? I do believe in them. I heard there are angels for different jobs. - Thanks, Irene

Dear Irene: When I started to get serious with my training in the metaphysical world and how to connect on a higher level, I started out reading everything I could about angels. I purchased many books on angels that seemed to speak to me. I then started my journey to find out about these beautiful beings who were created by God as his messengers.

We hear about angels stepping in to save someone from danger, and we see pictures of angels in churches and places that we visit, but there is so much more to learn. As a child, I found myself attracted to anything that had pictures of angels, and as I grew up and moved into my first apartment, I found myself buying statues of angels and placing one in each room where they could be seen. I seemed to find comfort in the knowledge that they seemed to be watching over me.

I would learn later that when we surround ourselves with pictures or statues of angels, they feel invited in, almost like a calling card of sorts to let them know we are open to being in their presence. So, as I started to learn more about each angel, I picked up a deck of angel cards as well. I would read about the angels every night before bed, bringing the book or angel cards with me, and putting them on my nightstand. This seemed to open a doorway for the angels.

Then night after night I would see angels as they appeared. I know this sounds unbelievable. It even amazed me.

I am frequently asked what does an angel look like? Very much like you or I, except sometimes I do see their wings.

Archangel Raphael is very much involved with me as he is a healer, and when I am giving a reiki session, he will occasionally show up beside the reiki bed and assist in healings.

That brings me back to the angel cards and your question. Start to work with the angels by showing them you are interested in working with them. Invite them into your home by placing statues near you, reading about them, or picking up a deck of angel cards and pulling one for yourself daily. You might not have the same experience as I had but don't give up. Have faith that your angels are always close to you and never far away.

Who Are Our Angels?

Often people wonder if a loved one who has passed could become an angel. As much as we may think of our loved ones who have passed as angels, and in our hearts they are, angels have never walked on Earth. Guardian angels are sometimes confused with "spirit guides." A spirit guide is a loving being who has lived on the Earth in human form. This person then received special training in the afterlife about how to become a spirit guide. Most spirit guides are deceased loved ones.

Guardian angels are a unique spiritual energy created by God, to do God's work on Earth and in Heaven. An angel may temporarily take the form of a person to do God's work or may take any form at all. As you know, there are no boundaries to God and how He may work his miracles. Every one of us is assigned a guardian angel that stays with us from birth throughout our lifetime until we return home to Heaven.

Archangels are the angels who supervise the guardian angels and angels upon the Earth. You can call upon an archangel whenever you need powerful and immediate assistance. Never think that your problem is too small for an archangel, or that you are somehow taking away from another person by calling on them. Archangels are not constrained by the space or time boundaries on Earth, and their assistance and love energy are endless.

Who are our archangels?

The word archangel comes from the Greek words 'architect' and 'angel' or 'chief angel'. Archangels watch over the guardian angels and specialize in specific human conditions.

The archangels are Michael, the first angel created by God, leader of all archangels and patron of police officers; Raphael, a powerful healer (as a reiki practitioner, I have seen Raphael lay his beautiful long white wings over someone who was in need of healing); Gabriel, the only archangel depicted as female in art and literature, Gabriel can bring messages to you just as she did to Elizabeth and Mary of the impending births of their sons, John the Baptist and Jesus of Nazareth; Uriel, considered one of the wisest archangels, Uriel warned Noah of the impending flood; Chamuel, the archangel of pure love, can lift you from the depths of sorrow and find love in your heart; and Jophiel, the angel present in the Garden of Eden.

What are some signs that angels are near?

There are many ways angels can make their presence known to us. We just need to look for the signs. These signs can sometimes be very subtle, but angels will always try to let you know they are close. You may see sparkles of light or flashes of color out of your peripheral vision. You may see feathers that seem to float down out of nowhere. You may hear a soothing whisper in your ear or a loud shout to warn you of danger.

Many times, it can be a light, comforting touch or just a sense that someone is with you. Or you might notice a sequence of numbers that normally would not appear together. These numbers will appear over and over, in the most unexpected ways and places, until you "get the message."

How do I communicate with my angels?

The best way to communicate or call forth your angels is for you to invite them to come to you. Give them a task. If it is in alignment with your highest and greatest good, they will work with you. We all have God's free will, and the angels will not step in and take control unless it is a life-or-death situation, and it is not your time to pass.

But if you ask for help, this is like music to their ears. It truly is their pleasure to assist you. When you meditate or otherwise quiet your mind, your angels are better able to communicate with you. That's why so many of us receive our angel messages right before we fall asleep or wake up, or when we are alone, doing something that does not require intensive thought or focus.

We All Have a Guardian Angel

Our guardian angels are assigned to us from birth and never leave us. Angels are pure light beings sent directly from God.

An archangel, such as Gabriel, will come to us as a form of additional guidance, inspiration, and protection when needed or called. They are not assigned to each of us at birth. Instead, these amazing beings can be omnipresent. Never be hesitant to call upon an archangel because you feel you are taking them away from larger problems! It is their sacred honor to help you.

A spirit guide is also typically assigned at birth, and your primary guide will stay with you throughout life. A spirit guide has typically walked on Earth previously, although they are not usually our loved ones or relatives who have passed on. Your guides bring the wisdom and perspective of many lifetimes and are simply there to help you.

Lastly, ascended masters surround us in our time of need. Ascended masters have also had previous incarnations as humans on Earth. Some of them are immediately recognizable from their lifetime as enlightened spiritual teachers, like Jesus or the Buddha.

As with many things in the spiritual realm, I've found that there are "levels" to ascended masters, too. For example, Jesus works miracles, and I've found him to be the divine healer of all ailments, both physical and spiritual. He is among the greatest of ascended masters.

But if, for instance, you wanted to patent an invention, you may want to call upon an ascended master who, in his earthly life, shone particularly strong in that field. In this example, you might want to call upon Thomas Edison. Ascended masters can be seen as "experts" who carried their specific areas of expertise with them into the afterlife.

My ascended master story is a fun one! One evening, before bed, I was reading one of Sylvia Browne's books. You may have known of Sylvia Browne as one of the more prominent television psychic mediums in the 1990s. As I was reading her book, I was also worrying about speaking publicly at one of my first demonstrations of psychic mediumship.

Believe it or not, I had stage fright and could just clam up when handed a microphone! I put the book down and went to bed.

That night, a younger man appeared in my dreams. He was African American, had this big afro, was wearing all these beaded necklaces, and looked like he was right out of the 1960s. He seemed to be telling me not to worry about the stage fright. I asked him who he was, and I heard, "JIMI!" shouted in response. I said, "Jimi who?" and heard back, "JIMI HENDRIX!" Then I heard, "Page 61!"

Now, I grew up in small-town Winchendon and had no idea who Jimi Hendrix was. I woke up my husband, George, from a sound sleep and asked him, poor guy! He muttered something about an electric guitarist and went back to sleep.

The next morning, I turned to Page 61 of Sylvia Browne's book, and to my amazement, discovered it detailed that Jimi Hendrix had terrible stage fright when he first began performing live and would clam up when handed a microphone, too!

Practice helped Hendrix become more comfortable. So, I started by simply speaking into an unplugged microphone in front of George, then gradually expanded to speaking in front of more family members and friends. Eventually, I was comfortable speaking in front of a large gathering, into a microphone.

And so, before all my group readings and large events now, I say a silent "thank you" to an unexpected, ascended master, the great Jimi Hendrix!

Angel Signs

Dear Bonnie: I have been going through some really tough times lately where I have felt very lost and alone. I started to catch on that I was receiving signs, and I am wondering if you could shed some light on what's going on. I am spiritual but I have never had so many coincidences. I know our loved ones can send signs as well, but these signs seem different. At times I feel as though I am getting a big hug from Heaven, and it brings me a lot of peace. At other times I see numbers and flashes of light. Who could this be? – Tommy

Dear Tommy: This sounds like you are receiving signs from the angelic realm. You see that angels are God's messengers. If you have been having a particularly tough time lately the angels are probably trying their best to get a message to you.

Some of the ways they do that are:

Numbers — Usually angel numbers are 111 or 222, 333, etc. This is only one of the ways angels talk to us. There are many meanings of angel numbers especially if they are in sequence.

If you start to notice upon waking up the clock says 1:11 and then you go to the grocery store and your receipt comes to $111.00, then start to look and notice these signs. The angels might be asking you to watch your thoughts, as thoughts are energy, and what we let come into our minds often enough is what we are going to manifest more of.

So, if you catch yourself thinking some negative thoughts like I am not good enough, I'm too heavy, or I don't fit in, then these thoughts now have a place in your mind. Learn to kick those thoughts to the side by acknowledging them and then giving them a positive spin. The angels ask you to turn these negative thoughts into positive thoughts with the knowledge that you are loved unconditionally, and the angelic realm wants nothing but the best for you.

Lights — If you are seeing lights, sparkling lights either with your eyes open or closed, these could be your angels acknowledging that they are surrounding you with love. They might be little sparkles or even streaks of light. Some people see different colored lights and can see the image of an angel. Different angels are known to show up with different colors surrounding them.

Archangel Michael has a deep blue or almost purple color surrounding him while Archangel Raphael, who is the healer, is associated with green. If you are seeing lights and you know it's not an eye condition, it's your angels letting you know they are surrounding you with love and guidance, and often healing heart, mind, and soul.

Feelings — I remember walking in the mall one day and feeling this bliss surround my entire being. I have never felt so loved. I remember saying to myself, wow, I wish I felt like this every moment. It was like I was getting a big hug from Heaven. Angels can come close and actually put their wings around you as if they are giving you a big hug. I am a reiki practitioner, and when I am giving a session, I will sometimes see an angel lay their wings over the entire length of my client. I soon realized my clients were usually aware of this feeling and knew the angels were near. Sometimes we just need that feeling that comes from a hug, a feeling of pure bliss.

Finding feathers — Have you been finding feathers in places that are out of the ordinary? I love finding feathers and I know a lot of other people do, as they certainly associate feathers with angels.

There are so many ways the angelic realm is trying to support you. Look for the signs as they are everywhere.

Don't Worry — Your Angels Are Still with You

Dear Bonnie: As a child, around the age of three, I saw angels for the first time that I can remember. I remember angels visiting me several times in the house my family lived in until I was about four. My mom also remembers waking me up from a nap, and when I awoke, I asked her, "Why did you wake me? I was playing with the angels." They always made me feel safe and protected; they had such an aura around them, transparent like fog but not cloudy. They appeared to be male, and they wore white. They were also so bright but, oddly, not blinding.

I have had other encounters, but none since I was much younger. I am writing to you and giving you this history because I feel like I have lost my sensitivity to see and feel things I was able to see as a child. Is there anything I can do to tap back into my abilities? — Sarah

Dear Sarah: As children, we can see and hear the spiritual world more easily and without effort. We have only been on the Earth plane for a short time and truly remember Heaven much more vividly. As we become older, that sensitivity can seem to go away because we must be on our Earth journey.

We all have a purpose for our lifetime, with many lessons to learn. And if we remembered everything about the journey that we came here to experience, then that might get in the way of living and learning these lessons with all the trials and tribulations that come with our lives.

You have not lost your sensitivity; life starts to unfold, and our journey begins. We start school to learn about science and math, which uses the other half of our brains, and the whimsical part of us becomes more scientific than magical.

Imagine if we were in a classroom, studying the alphabet or our math problems, and we kept seeing our angels all around us. That might not let us concentrate on the subjects we need to comprehend here in the physical world.

If you want to connect to the whimsical, creative side of yourself, try daydreaming when you get a chance. That's right, let your mind wander with no to-do list. Just for fun, sit in a comfortable chair and just let your mind take you to a carefree place where anything is possible. Think of how the great movies were made, like "Peter Pan." It all started with someone having whimsical thoughts.

Many great writers and artists will tell you that when they were not thinking, great inspiration came into their minds, and they wrote it down. We all are connected to source energy and are being inspired by guides, masters, and loved ones when we sleep and in our thoughts. The best way to connect then is to remember not to control your every thought. Just letting go and letting our minds wander can be so inspiring.

Meditation is also a great way to clear your mind of earthly matters. Just relaxing or listening to relaxing music can be beneficial in so many ways. If you choose to try meditation, set an intention: Ask the angels or your guides to come close and give you a sign or some advice that might be helpful to you.

Remember, don't try to run the show — just let things happen.

We are never alone on our journey and are always surrounded by so much love. We just need to take the time to enjoy the journey. Dream, meditate, let joy come into your world, and the journey will not seem so tough, and your ability to see, hear, and feel the spiritual world will not seem so far away.

Your Guides and Jesus

Your Guides have been assigned to you for a short time or a long time, depending on who they are and what role they play in your life. Some guides are with you for a specific reason or lesson that they are masters in and can offer you expertise in the same area that you might have wanted to learn or become an expert in yourself.

When I wanted to be better at public speaking, I would see myself in my Dreamtime standing on a stage with one of my guides, and they would be handing me the microphone. My brother, who became one of my spirit guides after his passing, was up on stage with me. Nothing that he would have done in his lifetime but in Heaven he took the time to get me comfortable on stage.

Jesus has shown himself to be one of my guides as well. I can see him and hear him as well. Jesus will come to you as you see him in movies or well-known pictures of him because he knows that you will recognize him this way. I love Jesus; can I just say that? When they say do as Jesus does it's for a really good reason.

Not only is he kind and compassionate, understanding and so much more, he shows himself in such a loving way, making you feel totally at ease and loved. I tell him all the time how cute he is, and he just smiles. His eyes are piercing, and his face is defined almost as a sculpture.

When I first started seeing him, he would be walking with Mary near a beautiful brook. My Native American guides have been with me from the beginning, one older and wiser and one who is young and tells me he is there to show me joy. He comes on a beautiful white horse and tells me to get on. He knows I love horses, but I have a fear of riding. He tells me you cannot get hurt here.

My Uncle Leon, who had passed away at the early age of 22, was one of my guides for many years. He was able to tell me it was him and he could psychically make my TV click on every time I walked in my room. One day as he did this, I said, "Okay, hotshot, I bet you cannot make the TV turn on," and as soon as I got those words out of my mouth, bam! The TV is totally on and blaring. It shocked me even though I asked for it, and I said out loud, "Okay, you can do it. That's enough." Then the TV went back to clicking.

Uncle Leon stayed with me for a long time, but our guides change when we need to grow. My great grandma Grace took over at that time and started walking me through my life going into my 40s. My grandmother, Birtha, and my great gramma Grace died very early in life and had not reached their 40s. I always wondered if I would, as I felt both of them strongly around me. I even have both of their pictures out where I can see them.

I started to feel Grace even stronger, and I was at a spiritualist church when another medium told me, "Your grandmother is always with you helping you to move past that mark of death before your 40's. She is carefully guiding and getting you past this age so you will grow older." I am not sure if this was written in our timelines that we would all pass young, but I did have a few scary moments when my life could have ended before the age of forty.

My Grandfather started to show up after that as a guide, maybe because I called to him. He passed when I was just two years old, but my mom would tell the story of him taking me and pulling my binky out of my mouth, saying, "She does not need this," and throwing it deep in the woods that surrounded our house. I liked that strongness about him, and as I dove into spiritualism, I wanted to get to know him for myself.

He had a bad reputation for drinking and being stern, but I felt a strong connection to him so one day I said out loud, "Grampa can I get a sign from you?" Suddenly, my two-story house seemed to smell of smoke! I thought my house was on fire and ran around trying to find the fire. There was nothing. Then when I stopped and listened inside my mind I heard, "You wanted a sign."

I called my mom, who was still alive, and asked her if Grampa had smoked. She said, "Does it smell strong like a cigar or pipe?" "Yes," I answered, and she replied, "Well, that's Grampa then." I would see Grampa after that in my Dreamtime and I always felt safe. He was stern still in Heaven, but I felt loved and protected.

My mother passed away three years before my father, and soon I would see Grampa with my mom, my brother in Heaven, and Jesus all together. They made quite a group of guides. My brother Dickie was the first to pass, and even though he was 15 years older than me, and we really didn't grow up together, I always looked up to him. He had a funny, strong sense of humor but was always gentle with me.

He also had a drinking problem that, as I know now, can easily be passed from one generation to another. He showed himself on a day of training I had gone to the Omega Institute in Rhinebeck, N.Y. I was bringing through a young daughter for two parents who came for the training. They wanted to learn how to connect. It was my first time learning how to connect with a loved one in Heaven, but it wasn't hard for me. My brother, who I could psychically see, stood beside me and was so amazed at what I could do. He kind of screamed in excitement. I had to say to him, "Hey, I am working!" But I was so excited he was there at the workshop with me, even from the other side.

You would have thought I wouldn't make him stay and work, but I did, and he did it gladly. When someone was having a hard time making a connection, I would ask him to be that spirit they were bringing through, and he always showed up as that redheaded kid with a fishing pole in his hand. After that Dickie would be at all the events and galleries where I would be demonstrating and giving me support.

One gallery was about to start, and I started to feel ill. I even said to myself they could refund everyone's money. Well, that didn't go well with Dickie, and I saw him come to my face as he said, "You better get out there or I'll give you a kick in the butt." I answered him back like a snotty little sister, "Then you'd better help me." I went into the gallery area, and I swear I gave the best readings with such humor, love, and accuracy I had ever given. Ask, and you shall receive.

Numbers from Heaven

Spirit will use many ways to get a message to you. It might be your angels, guides, or loved ones who want to let you know they are around you. It's usually when there might be a challenge or something new coming up that they want to give you a heads-up on or could even be just a hello from Heaven.

Here are some numbers and their meanings so if you keep receiving messages, this way you'll know what your spirit team wants you to know. Remember, when you see the numbers, always use your gut instinct to see if they have more of a message for you. By using your sixth sense, you will connect on a higher level and create a conversation.

1. You are manifesting what you are thinking about, so be careful with your thoughts. The number 1 always means a new beginning, so look for a gift from spirit that is being offered to you now. Now is the time to make a wish and co-create with the divine.
2. Twos are always about relationships. Time to pay attention to a relationship or partnership that might need your attention. We are happy in our lives when we are in loving, working relationships. Think of the person who always has your back.
3. Threes are about working together to bring harmonious outcomes. Spirit asks you to come together with people in your life and use your creativity to make things happen. It could mean two becoming three.
4. Fours are things that are coming together to make a solid foundation for your dreams and desires. The angels around you are helping you to manifest your desires and dreams.
5. Fives are all about change happening around you. Be on the lookout for these changes so you can deal with them positively. These changes will have you headed in the right direction.
6. Lots of harmony and balance around you at this time. The angels are there to celebrate with you now. You have overcome the challenges in your life and are now heading in the right direction.

7. Look at the past to see the future. See what has worked and things and situations that have not worked out so well and see what fits you now. Be aware that you are being guided in your choices at this time.
8. It's time to move forward, to manifest your dreams and desires. Prosperity in the things that mean the most to you is happening now. Ask help from those you trust to help with the manifesting. Happy times.
9. Nines are about your dreams and desires that are there for you to attain. These are plans about to come to fruition and the angels bringing forth good news. You are almost there; keep working at growing your business, finances, and relationships.
10. Tens are about culmination and happiness as you have come to the end of a cycle and completion. Your spirit team is saying, "Good for you." Your hard work and diligence have paid off, and the timing is right. You're surrounded with abundance in many ways.

I hope the meaning of these numbers helps you to connect to your spirit team and bring hope and joy into your life. We are never alone, so look for those signs around you.

My Native American Guide

Dear Bonnie: Do you believe everyone has a guide? I have been seeing a Native American in my dreams, and I am wondering how I can know if he is a guide and how I can build a relationship with him. — Thanks, Steve

Dear Steve: I too have a Native American as a guide. At first, I saw him as a young child. We lived out in a rural area in a small town, and I took the school bus back and forth to school. One day while getting off the bus and running toward the front door of my home I gazed over at our front porch to see a big Native American sitting on the front porch. I know my mouth dropped open as I could see his frame and face so clearly.

My mom, who also has the gift of clairvoyance (clear seeing), was looking at me at the same time. She could see him sitting there as well. The term for what my mother was doing is called "linking in". She could see what was happening and called out to me, saying, "It's all right. He waits for you to get off the bus every day."

Through the years, I would see this same man in my dream time as he would appear and show me his face, at times coming so close I could see the deep wrinkles that lined his face. I knew he was a man of significant importance and well-respected. Even though he seemed strong and silent, I knew he had a kind and loving heart.

One day while doing a meditation I slipped into a serene sense of peace, and as I came back to consciousness I could see him once again, but this time he seemed to be sitting. As he disappeared from my vision, I heard the word 'sitting'. Confused as to why he would leave me with those words, I continued with my day when the second word came: bull. I realized he was telling me his name was Sitting Bull.

Becoming excited as I realized who my guide was, I wanted to know more. I called my father and asked him if he knew the story of Sitting Bull and then Googled his name, wanting to know more about my lifetime guide. He has appeared through the years, showing me his face in my dream time or meditations to let me know he has stayed with me through the years.

I am not sure exactly why our guides choose us, but I have learned this from listening to the spirit world: it is a process that is not taken lightly. I recently watched a movie that just came out about the life of Sitting Bull and at the end of the film he dies. My heart became heavy with grief as I watched the history of his story.

That night, when I was in my dream time, I began to see tall trees and a forest. Soon, my guide appeared on his favorite white horse. He was riding through the woods, stopping his horse in front of me, letting me see his proud and strong face. He sent me these thoughts; he was with the Great Spirit in the spiritual world, and I knew he was reassuring me that he was okay and for me not to worry.

I do know each of us has a guide, sometimes more than one. They watch over our journey here on Earth. If you want to have a relationship with your guide, meditation is the number one way of connecting to them. There are many guided meditations for meeting your guides as well as just sitting in silence with the intention that one of your guides connect to you, and maybe even getting the name of your guide.

Remember to ask your guide his or her name before you start the meditation so your connection will become strong and you can feel comfortable calling to them when you need strength and protection, feeling their guidance on your journey.

How Can I Meet My Spirit Guide?

Your spirit guide is tightly bonded with you, making your time here as comfortable as your road can be while at the same time not stepping on your toes, as you have your own free will. If your path feels like it has been more bumpy than smooth, it could be that you chose harder lessons to learn or you might not be listening to the help that is there for you from your guide and your heavenly team trying to assist you.

How can you hear your guide better, you ask? Meditation is the number-one way to connect with your higher self and the team that is with you always. Meditation doesn't need to be complicated or ceremonial. It can be as easy as finding a quiet space where you will not be disturbed. The key is to quiet the mind, taking out your thoughts and leaving nothing but a blank screen.

Some like quiet, while others play soft music. It's really what works best for you: going out in nature, sitting on a rock or under a tree, wherever you can find peace. Others receive information easier if they are doing an active meditation, something that keeps you busy but at the same time does not take any active thinking. Going out for a walk or dancing around your living room could be the way you can connect.

I know when I am vacuuming, lots of ideas seem to flood my mind. I have learned to say, "Thank you," to the higher power, knowing these thoughts that come to my mind are not my own but those of my guides.

If you would like a closer relationship with your guide, set an intention of meeting your guide and letting him or her know you are ready to listen to his or her divine guidance. As you make the time to meditate, ask your guide to join you. If you can set aside some time each day, even if it's five minutes, your guides will be happy to have this time with you. It's like making a date with your guide.

As you begin to meditate, ask your guide to show you how its presence feels as it comes close. Empty your mind and begin to feel the feelings that are coming through. It might take a few times to feel the sensations or vibrations that will be your spirit guide's calling card.

If you want an intimate relationship with your guide, this time is needed to let that bond happen. The sensation as the guide comes closer might feel like goosebumps, your heart pounding, or just a feeling of peace. Don't try to rush it. Let the feelings come naturally. This is a way to start feeling and connecting to your guide.

Besides a sense of knowing your guide is near, you might be able to receive a picture or scene in your mind's eye or even a thought or voice inside your head. As you get used to calling in your guide, you will become aware of whether these are your thoughts or your guide getting a sign to you.

It takes time to build up a relationship with your guide, so be patient. When you feel comfortable knowing your guide is by your side, start asking questions that you would like answers to. They might not come that day but be on the lookout. Your guide is sure to be sending you the signs.

The Blueprint of Your Life

Dear Bonnie: Do you believe in spiritual guides? I feel like I have one that steps in and helps me when I need some direction. What are your thoughts? — Laurie

Dear Laurie: Yes, I very much believe in guides, and I can tell you that you have many guides around you at this moment.

Before you came down to Earth, you met with your spirit guides to design a blueprint for your life, a blueprint that would enable your soul to have many learning opportunities so your soul could grow and evolve. Life is our schoolroom for learning, so our guides help us decide which path would be the best for us at this time.

You chose the existence that is yours today, and your guides helped with choosing your soul family of which to be a part. You are never left alone, as your guides are an important part of your journey. It's so rewarding to meet our team of helpers on the other side.

Meditation and dream time are two of the ways that you can learn to connect with them. Your guides are your spiritual teachers. They give you guidance, knowledge, and wisdom. Angels, family members, ancestors, ascended masters and teachers are just a few who become our guides.

Guides help us fulfill the spiritual contract you made before your trip to Earth this time around. Some guides stay with us throughout our entire lives until we are home again, and some are specialty guides that pop in to help with a project or when we need help learning something new.

When I was teaching a dance class many years ago, I would go to bed knowing I had to have the steps down by the next morning, and I would often, during my dream time, see dancers in heaven helping me with the steps.

If you are not seeing your guides, do not become worried; they are there and are very committed to making sure your life journey is going as planned. They cannot change our free will but are behind the scenes sending us signals that they are around with love and guidance.

It's our job to pay attention to the signs they are sending. Have you ever found a white feather where there is no logical reason for it to appear?

Your loved ones, who step into the role of your guides, may have met you or not, but are a part of your teaching and guiding team. You may sense them in many ways.

Nature plays a big part when they are letting you know they are around. Birds, clouds, rainbows, shooting stars, butterflies and more can all be signs that your loved ones are close by and offering comfort and guidance. It's our job to watch for these signs and pay attention to the world around us every day so we can become one with our guides.

When you make the connection to your guides, you will never feel alone on your journey, making life a little easier even if you are on the road less traveled.

Animal Spirit Guides

Dear Bonnie: I have been repeatedly having the same dream of a deer that makes itself known to me. It just stands there looking at me. Do you think there is a message for me? I have heard of spirit animals but how do you find out what they want you to know? — Thanks, Robert

Dear Robert: Thanks for the question, Robert. I recently posted a picture of eight does on my back lawn. They were something I had never seen before. Someone stated, "Wow. I wonder what a deer means as a spirit animal." What's a spirit animal? A spirit animal is identified as a teacher or messenger from the divine. They are meant to bring you a specific message and are seen as signs from above.

We all have guides and master guides that try to send us signs with a message about something that is going on in our lives. They help you on your journey here on Earth by offering you guidance. Your spirit animal helps with life lessons, and as the guide, they help you through these lessons with their unique nature and their abilities.

How can you connect with your spirit animals? Start with having complete faith and belief in the spirit realm and through a knowing inside your heart your spirit animal will find you. Some of the ways your spirit animal will find you — because we do not find them, they find us — are in dreams. The number-one way the spirit realm collaborates with us is in our dream time. So, if you are dreaming of a particular spirit animal, it has a message for you.

Another way to connect and find your spirit animal is to be out in nature. Be aware of what animals or birds appear to you. That skunk or porcupine that crosses your path may have a meaning.

Meditation is a wonderful way to call to the spirit realm and your spirit animal. Asking them to appear and then asking them what their message is for you is a wonderful way to get to know who is guiding you.

Visions, dreams, and finding your spirit animal in its life form are all there for you.

What does your spirit animal want you to know?

Insight into your life.

They are keeping you connected to a higher power than yourself, which is always looking out for your best interest. They are there to protect you, guide you, and keep you on your life's path.

Now what does a deer symbolize? Kindness, gentleness, an innocence with peace and serenity. If the deer has found you it's because you are gentle but not completely defenseless. A deer tells you to be strong, but in a gentle way, with a situation going on in your life.

You are likely seeing the deer because you are in tune with the inner child within you. Make sure you honor that inner child within yourself. A deer can also mean alertness, vigilance, and flexibility. Deer can hear what is not being said and can feel what is not being demonstrated in your life.

On the spiritual side, a deer symbolizes that this might be the time for you to trust your intuition and psychic abilities so you can reach further with your abilities to use your abilities with ease and to know when you need or want these abilities. Have confidence that even though you are gentle you have strong abilities that can help others on their path.

Our Soul Family

Before we came to Earth, our soul family (those who reincarnate with us again and again in many lifetimes) sat down with the masters and guides and decided what each one of us wanted to learn this time around to experience different circumstances that would let our souls expand and grow.

There is a blueprint of our lives, a plan of experiences and circumstances that we want to experience, but indeed not the choices we make, for each one of us has free will. If we didn't, we might be happier with everything always going our way, but there would be no lessons to be learned, and we might all look and act like puppets, which is not intended for us.

Each soul comes here with the knowledge that life here will be difficult, with many lessons to be learned as a way of letting our soul expand and grow. When we accept the trials and tribulations that are given to us, and they are not just endured, we come to realize there is a lesson in everything that happens in this lifetime.

Love is the reason for our existence, and by learning to love with an unconditional love that has no prejudice and knowing that everything is just as it is supposed to be, we live with the knowledge that each lesson is meant as a way to personal growth.

Your soul family that came here this time with you may have decided they did not want to live long lives, or their free will of life choices could have hurried them back to heaven sooner than expected. Without the full knowledge of each situation, I can only assume you are here to learn lessons that you have chosen for yourself.

A young life going back home could be that person's choice, or the lesson might be yours to learn. I am sure that with each passing you had to learn to be stronger without the person you depended on and assumed would be here with you much longer. Sympathy and compassion reflect the growth of your soul, as each passing brought about these two things. It is not easy living in a world where everything is not a given, but only a blessing, and sometimes just for a short while.

I know it's not always easy to see the bright side of things, but if you strive to live a life trusting the process and having faith in your heart, living this time on Earth might be a little easier. Face every day as a new beginning and try to see the beauty in every new blessing and pain, knowing that each situation is a chance to see your soul's growth.

When we start to embrace and not fear our journey, the change in our attitudes can be amazing. Trust in God and have faith, believing that there is a plan and that we are being guided and loved from above, knowing we will see and be with those who love us once again.

You Only Get One Soul

Dear Bonnie: I used to feel so happy, and as I have grown older life seems to have kicked me in the butt. How do I get back to a place of feeling connected to God and spirit and start to feel grounded again? — Bailey

Dear Baily: One thing we need to do as we go through life is to make sure we don't let the troubles of the world weigh us down to the point of losing or dimming our inner light. Your inner light is a gift to you that is meant to shine bright. We are born with this light inside of us when we come into the world.

You can close your eyes and bring yourself back to a simpler time around the age of five or six and picture yourself standing in a field of flowers or inside your family home. See that little girl or boy with that smile on your face, knowing that you are connected and safe. Your innocent soul is not yet aware of the things on Earth that are hard, like feeling the pressure of earning a living or making sure dinner is on the table, or even the feeling of not being enough or having enough, the childlike existence of just wanting to be loved and cared for and full of joy as you play.

Life can seem to burn out that shining light of hope and the fearlessness we have when we are born. The soul comes to Earth with a purpose for this lifetime. We feel fulfilled when we are on that path, but if we have strayed, either by giving up a dream because it seemed frivolous to the world or our parents, or because the opportunities didn't appear for us, we might forget why we are here on this journey called life.

We bend our dreams so they fit into a box of what we think we are supposed to be doing and forget the childlike instinct to enjoy the now and look for the fun. We ignore that gut feeling of taking classes in school that we might enjoy and excel in because they might not get us a job that makes a certain amount of money, and we have a fear of not meeting others' standards.

When we come from a place of fear and not love, we are ignoring our inner light. We replace it with a 'what if'. We have two choices in life: we can be fear-based or love-based. Those are the only two choices: love or fear. Our ego tries to keep us safe by becoming fear-based but limits how high we can fly and bring our dreams to fruition.

Love can be scary at times but so worth the chance of happiness. If you take a chance and it doesn't work in your favor, at least you tried. Keep trying until you get that promotion, job, or relationship you have been searching for. You are meant to have a fulfilling life full of joy.

My advice is to shine your light as brightly as you can, let go of fear, and ask yourself what your six-year-old self would want. We are only here for a short time. Why not live with the enthusiasm of our young soul that has so many plans and dreams? Always come from a place of love, not fear. Take care of your soul. You only have one.

Can You Find Another Soulmate?

Dear Bonnie: I recently broke up with my boyfriend. He says we are soulmates and wants to continue the relationship, but I believe the relationship has run its course. If he is my soulmate, does that mean I won't find someone new? — Elissa

Dear Elissa: I believe we have many soulmates and even a soul family. We come down to Earth each time we reincarnate with our soul family so that we can teach and learn valuable lessons. In our new-age way of thinking, if you have met your soulmate everything should be perfect, and we are meant to be together forever.

That sounds like a fairy tale to me, but it does sound nice.

The truth is that each person in our life is here to teach us a lesson our soul needs to learn to grow and expand, becoming more enlightened each time. When this lesson is learned, the relationship could move on or change when the mission is accomplished. Some relationships are meant to last a lifetime while others just a short time. Each relationship we have offers something new and challenging.

Think back to the time you first met your boyfriend. What drew you to him? There was an attraction for a reason, something that made your heart swell and made you know you were meant to be with this person. Ask yourself, what has this person taught me since I committed to be in this relationship? If the lessons have been learned and the spark has seemed to have fizzled, maybe both of you have done your part.

It's a good idea before leaving any relationship to look at the big picture and view each side. It is not possible to go through life without having a few bruises and bumps along the way.

Here is an exercise that would help both of you to move on with love and compassion, which is a lesson on its own. In each relationship in our lives, cords of energy can be attached to each person. Cords are not always negative energy. They can also be from those we love. Cutting these cords and sending them back can free your own emotions and help the other person, as well, to feel whole and loved without clinging to your energy.

Try this: sitting back in a comfortable chair, holding onto a piece of rose quartz crystal (the crystal related to the heart chakra), sitting with soft music playing, and begin to feel yourself becoming relaxed. Call in your guardian angel and ask them to give you a sign that they are nearby. Feel yourself receiving a gentle hug. Feel the love and affection the angel has for you.

Now, going down to the center of your chest to your heart, feel your heart beginning to fill with love. Send healing energy to your heart and picture a pink ball of light shining brightly. Now picture the person who has hurt your feelings or wounded your heart, someone you would like to release from your energy field.

Allow the healing energy to go to the person you are seeing in your mind's eye.

See the connection between the two of you. See the cords that have been attached between you. These cords can look and feel very different, some lighter, some darker, thicker, or some appearing thin like spaghetti. Ask your guardian angel to remove any painful cords, leaving only the love you feel for each other.

Ask that any lasting emotions or thoughts be taken up to heaven and the higher side of life. Give yourself some time to do this. Ask the angels to help you move forward in your life and to see only the best in the person you are leaving or have an attachment to.

Be free to love again and live each day with love and compassion and have a heart that is filled with love for yourself and others. We are meant to live a joyous life filled with love.

Search Your Soul

Dear Bonnie: Do you believe we have soul lessons? Are these predetermined and, if so, can we make choices, so the lessons are easily received? It seems some of the lessons that have been showing up in my life are hard to handle. —Ann

Dear Ann: We are a soul having a human experience. I heard this statement from my years of training in the metaphysical world, but I don't think I truly knew what that meant until one night while sleeping, I was shown how our souls look on the other side.

Before an event one night, I was shown souls waiting in line in Heaven to be at the event the next evening, waiting patiently for me to deliver messages to their loved ones. When I see clairvoyantly in my third eye, I always have seen loved ones who look just like they did while they were here on Earth, but this one night they wanted me to see them as souls.

To my surprise, I could see bright, beautiful lights with what seemed to be frames of bodies. I didn't see clothing or faces and details of people, as I usually see, just these beautiful souls letting me know they were not going to let me down, they would be there for the show.

Although I loved being shown this beautiful sight, I sent a thought to the spirit world: I love seeing you as you were here in the physical world. Since then, that's how I see everyone in heaven.

We are souls that come down from heaven with the intention of learning lessons that we have decided, with our guides and masters, would enhance and grow our souls and make a learning experience.

The exact way these lessons are to be learned is not told to us. Otherwise, we would wait for these lessons to unfold, taking away the opportunity for growth. Life is just our schoolroom or classroom where the lessons can be learned from trials and obstacles that seem to be getting in our way.

Many think, why is this happening to me? Depending on how you view each situation that comes into your life, lessons may seem daunting and draining. Taking a look at each difficult experience with the knowledge that there is a lesson that can be a teaching opportunity and looking at each problematic situation in this way can take away some of the anxiety that might come from having the problem.

See each situation that seems challenging as a learning tool, and ask yourself, what lesson can I learn from this experience? Lessons are in our lives to help not hurt us. So, if we can embrace each day and try to understand to take each day as an opportunity to add to our soul's growth instead of seeing events as challenges, life seems to run a little smoother.

Recognize and acknowledge the lesson and then say, "Thank you," and let it go with grace. Only then can the lesson go away.

Your Soul's Evolution

We go through the process of looking at where our soul could grow and the experiences necessary for our soul growth. Past-life karma is looked at and evaluated on many levels. Your soul wants to experience many different scenarios with families, economic conditions, poor to rich or vice versa, social status, spiritual and individuals' beliefs. Your soul goes through many lifetimes in the hope of spiritual and soul growth.

Your soul evolution is looked at and the planning starts. Figuring out the needs for growth, your guides, teachers, and you, will look at many scenarios and choose the one that will fit you best. It's like watching many movies and choosing the one that you want to be in.

It's hard to imagine that we choose the life we are currently in, but that's the way it works. You chose your parents, siblings (yes, your siblings), the circumstances that create your world now. If you look at each adventure or mishap that has happened in your life you can take on a new outlook.

Ask yourself how you can lovingly handle each situation, knowing there is a lesson to be learned and you did indeed choose to learn it.

Can you believe you choose your body: what type of body male or female, handicapped, gorgeous, not-so-attractive, all with lessons to learn? Imagine being a model or actress who is judged by their appearance, constantly having to submit themselves to the judgment of onlookers. Maybe the lesson they came with is to find the beauty within themselves and not be burdened with what others think or say about them.

Imagine wanting to be born with a disability so you might teach others compassion.

When it's time to reincarnate it is totally up to you to choose. You might wait until your soul family is ready to reincarnate with you. Your soul family can include your parents, siblings, co-workers, family, and friends. I know my husband and I have been together in many lifetimes and many different scenarios. One time he was even my redheaded brother.

After my father passed last year, I kept asking the question of why this was the hardest experience I have gone through. My dad was my dad, but we had such an understanding of each other that there was not one moment of unrest with us. Never once was I mad at my father for anything. Hard to believe, but we had an all-knowing ability with each other that never ended. After his passing, I started to ask questions of spirit and received the answer that we had been through many lifetimes together and would be again.

I was certainly here this time to show him the meaning of unconditional love, as he was for me.

When we reincarnate, we forget all the other lives we have lived and what lessons we choose for this lifetime, but that's only so we can have a fresh start this time around and experience all the joy and sorrows that we may encounter for our soul's growth.

Enjoy life and find the joy that is ours. Let go of hurts, anger slowly, and laugh a lot. Earth is just our schoolroom, not where we will live forever.

Your Soul's Journey

Dear Bonnie: Why does it seem like some have everything and others not enough? — Kimmy

Dear Kimmy: There's a saying that's been out there for a long time; "The only two things you can be sure of are taxes and dying." But in the meantime, there is a lot of life to go through. Your soul came to Earth this time around to experience something or someone that it needed in order to grow, expand, and become more aware.

Have you ever had that feeling of 'I know there must be more'? I think we start to ask ourselves this when we are on our journey. It's going fine, but something deep inside of us knows that something is missing.

Our soul picks who our parents are going to be. Yes, that's right. You picked your mom and dad and the circumstances that you were born into before coming into your Earthly situation. Some chose to be born into rich and famous households while others were born into middle-class families that appear to look like a Norman Rockwell painting.

Then there's the hard-working family that works all the time but never seems to have enough to go around. There are other situations that are far worse than these, and you wonder why any soul would want to come down to Earth and live this existence. It's the hardest situations that offer the most growth.

There is learning and growth in each situation that life will bring us through, both the good and the bad. My mom always told me the grass isn't always greener on the other side. Each of us has his own journey, and sometimes we ponder why our life or situation is the way it is. I have always told my son since he was little that there are always going to be others who have less than you and others who have more.

Your soul has been here many times before. Its mission is to experience different situations, and it has chosen your life the way it is this time on Earth so it can learn from these different experiences: rich, poor, famous, or an average Joe, hopefully becoming more sympathetic or open-hearted as your soul goes through each situation.

The goal, I believe, is to be at peace with what you have and to be able to understand another's point of view. Can you see someone else's point of view without letting it take the peace inside you? Remember that we are here for just a short time, and this is our schoolhouse. We are here to learn, and sometimes it's a challenge.

The next time you are facing a challenge, look at the difficulty from a bird's-eye view and ask yourself, "What is my lesson? What did I want to learn when I chose to come to Earth in my current situation?" By looking at obstacles from a different perspective, you might be able to see the lesson.

When we learn to grow with each new experience, good or bad, our soul is expanding. With each situation you are going through, there is a new opportunity for growth. Take a deep breath, and trust that it will be okay in the end, no matter what the outcome might be.

If you move past and learn from all that is going on around you and face the challenges with a knowing from deep inside that this, too, is a growth spurt, it might take away the fear or worry. Face what you fear and handle the problem from a loving point of view and notice that the problem or challenge will soon dissipate.

Sometimes we just need to feel that we are enough.

Your Soul's Purpose

Do you believe our souls have a purpose and, if so, why is it so hard to find out what it is? I am having a tough time at my workplace, and I am wondering if that's what I am meant to be doing.

Sometimes when the universe, the divine, or your guides are trying to get a message to you, the lessons may seem tough. In your case, the job that you are performing may not be your soul's path. When we choose to come here to have an Earth experience, we choose a blueprint to follow. We always choose a job or career that will fulfill our destiny and open ourselves up for our soul's growth. If the job you are in now does not feel rewarding to you any longer, it may be time to ask yourself what would make you happy.

The universe always wants us to be enjoying our time here on earth, so when they make things difficult it usually means it's time to move forward. If your job were still satisfying to you, you wouldn't have these feelings of 'is there any more than this?' It might be time to ask yourself, "What would bring me joy and still make the money I need to pay my bills?"

Dig in deep and ask yourself what you believe you are supposed to be doing for work. Where does your interest lie? What makes your heart fill with excitement when you think of doing this job all day long or even part-time? Think about what comes naturally to you. Are you good with children? Animals? Writing? Then think of how you could use your talents to bring in the money you need while at the same time fulfilling your soul's purpose.

Your soul purpose usually involves helping others in some way. We are all born with different talents; it's a given. Whether we choose to grow these talents and use them to make the world a better place is up to us. It comes with our free will that no one can take away.

Our talents can come with challenges that we may need to overcome, such as the person who has a beautiful voice but is too scared to stand in front of an audience or the person who feels everyone is better than them at their trade. When we overcome our hang-ups and insecurities, our true selves can shine. It might take some work if you lack self-confidence, but it sure will be worth it in the end to see the results of your hard work.

Going out of your comfort zone to try new things is not easy, and that's when you want to ask for help. If it was meant to be and you're putting in the work, it will happen. Our jobs take up a lot of our time here on earth, so make sure you are satisfied with what you are doing and not just playing it safe. Life is for having faith and taking chances.

I am not saying quit your job and wait for a miracle, but what I am saying is start to take action towards your goal. When you put your energy into making things happen you will start to manifest what you truly desire. If you need to start small by taking classes or finding a mentor, start there. Life should be about enjoying our time here and at the same time helping others along the way.

Your Higher Self

Dear Bonnie: I have so many ideas that float around inside my mind that are promising ideas about work or how to make my dreams and plans for my life happen, and I take a mental note to acknowledge them but then get distracted. Then I go on to something new, never putting my thoughts into action. How can I stop doing this and where are these thoughts and ideas coming from?

Dear Mary: Many of us hear thoughts that come and go in our minds. When I was little, I wondered if everyone was always having a conversation with themselves like I seemed to be having. It was like having a friend to talk to. I now know that it is my higher self talking back to me.

What is your higher self? It is the absolute best of you which lives in your soul. We all are souls having a physical experience here on Earth, but first and last, you are a soul being.

Our soul chooses to come into the physical plane and have an Earthly experience to learn many new lessons but also to carry out its purpose. What is your soul's purpose? We came into this lifetime for the experience and desire to learn something new or feel and act differently than the last reincarnation, a chance for the soul to expand and grow. We learn new ways of dealing with life.

Your soul's purpose is to accept and love yourself and, at the same time, learn how to develop into a better and more understanding person. The soul's purpose usually involves opening up to the realization that we are all one with each other and that we must learn how to help others and humankind.

We are given many chances to become one with our higher selves and realize what love and life are all about and how we can become all that we are meant to be. I believe it starts with self-love and how we feel about ourselves.

That is why we have that little inner voice always asking us to do the very best thing for ourselves and others, that small voice that always tells you the other person's side of the story when you get angry at a friend or family member, the little voice that comes from the absolute best of you that never has a negative thought or feeling, but tries to make you see the true meaning of what is happening around you.

So why are all these thoughts and ideas running around your head, but then you never act upon them? Well, that is up to you to do the work, and your own free will kicking in. We can hear thoughts of help, hope, or creative ideas, but might never follow up on them.

So, if you hear thoughts for you to move ahead on a new job, a new relationship, or a creative idea, they all could lead you to success, but that would take you having that conversation within yourself. My dad used to say, "You can lead a horse to water, but you cannot make it drink."

If you are receiving guidance from your higher self, try listening and then writing down your ideas. Take even small steps, one at a time, in the direction you wish to see happening in your life. Make sure not to listen to any negative thoughts that pop up, like you're too old to do that or not smart enough or as pretty as someone else, because that's just your EGO talking. EGO stands for Edging God Out.

No one wants to see you fail, so make a plan and learn to listen to that inner voice that loves you and wants nothing but for you to succeed.

What's Heaven Like?

Last week, I took another poll on my Facebook page asking, "What does heaven look like?" Your responses painted a picture of a beautiful, joyful place surrounded by our loved ones.

Once, when I was driving through falling snow, I heard a voice tell me that the snow, swirling around my car and sparkling, looked like what surrounds us as we transition into heaven. It was peaceful and so very beautiful. People who have had near-death experiences often report that they saw or felt surrounded by a beautiful white, shimmering light, sometimes appearing as a tunnel.

Heaven, I think, can be what you make it. It's another dimension, another plane of existence, and certainly not carved in stone. Things take on an energetic identity, like a hologram, rather than the dense physical characteristics they'd have here on Earth.

Clairvoyants, like me, can translate this energy into a psychic vision, which they can then use to identify a loved one to a client in a reading. The loved one might be doing something or wearing something in particular which I'll use to further identify the energy.

The sky's the limit in Heaven! Whatever your loved one can think of, he or she can energetically manifest in a moment. Whether it's joining you across the world in spirit or participating again in their favorite activity when they were alive, anything's possible for those in heaven.

Some of my Facebook friends commented that they believe heaven to be full of nature, completely unspoiled, in heightened, vibrant colors. If their Heaven is a field, it is a field filled with the most fragrant, fully blossomed flowers and soft, emerald-green grass. If their Heaven is a beach, the sand shimmers like diamonds and the water is the perfect blue.

In all of these visions of heaven my Facebook friends included their loved ones who had passed, mentioning their pets and even people who were not related, but close friends and neighbors. They found Heaven to be a place of nonjudgment and peace, compassionate and loving.

Our loved ones who had passed from illness or old age are healthy, whole, and young again in heaven. When I do a reading for a client, their loved one may at first appear to me how the client last knew them. The loved one does this purposefully, so the client can easily identify them. As the reading goes on, gradually the loved one will return to the appearance in which they feel best. They may look younger, healthier, or simply wear clothing or accessories that were meaningful to them in life.

Even our pets who have passed on do this! I have seen an elderly dog transform into a puppy and dreamed of an arthritic dog I had, bounding joyfully through a grassy field in heaven. It's so wonderful to see all of God's creations looking and feeling their best again, especially after an illness.

And I can promise you this: When we pass, none of us goes alone. Even if a person passes where there is not another living person beside him, his spiritual team surrounds him. As our vital signs begin to fade, our guardian angels, guides, and loved ones who have passed step in to accompany us energetically. Even those who are living can feel an energetic shift in the room, to one of peace and acceptance. Our spiritual team leads us through the transition and encourages us thoroughly along the way.

Heaven is right here beside us. It's simply in a dimension invisible to most eyes. And that is why those who have died never leave us. Consciousness is never lost; it is transformed. Thoughts become tangible things, and vice versa. Your reality on Earth can be whatever you choose to manifest, and your Heaven can be just as real.

Picturing Heaven

Dear Bonnie: I want to be able to picture Heaven. What do you think my loved ones are doing in Heaven after they pass? Do you get a glimpse of what Heaven looks like when you are conducting a reading? Thanks, Bev

Dear Bev: After over a decade of delivering messages from the other side, I can receive information and get a view into what your loved ones are doing on the other side. The funny thing is that your loved ones are usually doing what they loved doing here on their time on earth.

When I deliver messages to my clients, I often hear the soul coming through with messages such as 'tell my mom I am still skiing,' and I will get a visual of their son skiing on a mountain. And the client will tell me, yes, that was one of her son's hobbies.

And, yes, they have mountains in Heaven. Your Heaven will be the best version of your life on Earth. I often pull a card from my Messages from Heaven oracle deck that I created, and the message will often be that I can do everything in Heaven that I liked doing here on Earth.

It took me a while to understand what creating our own version of Heaven really means. Mine would not be skiing on a cold winter's day in the mountains, but this young man's version of Heaven was just that. I often see my dad riding horses in Heaven, and I once sent a thought up to him as to this fact, and he answered, "That is not all I do."

I have learned that not only do we play sports or participate in card games, but we might even be watching our favorite shows on TV, and we also many times have jobs. They would not be jobs that were not your passion or your calling but rather jobs that would be of service to someone here on Earth, and you would feel passionate about it. Watching over family members who are still living is also something we usually do as well in Heaven.

If you were a scientist here and you passed to the higher side of life, you might want to watch over and inspire other scientists trying to help the world. For instance, if you were a specialist in a specific field, you may take on the job of helping those in that field.

In other words, you can help others here on Earth and are able to enjoy everything you enjoyed while you were on your journey here. Now, I am sure that all that work comes from your soul's evolution of learning and helping others. My uncle, who was in the Army, showed me he welcomes home soldiers who have passed suddenly and who have died while in a war. He greets them in a special room in Heaven and makes them feel safe, letting them know they are not alone.

I advise everyone here on their journey on earth to enjoy life's pleasures. If you like to go to the beach, do that. If you like to play in the snow, then go for it. If educating yourself gives you joy, sit and read or listen to an audiobook. Just follow your heart.

It is not the things that we collect on Earth. It is our memories and experiences and, of course, the people we bring to the higher side of life. Heaven is a continuous evolution of our soul. Keep learning and growing here, and that's what you bring with you when you pass – that and the love in your heart.

When you imagine your loved one in Heaven, picture them doing their favorite things and keep them close to your heart as they are never far away and very much still living life.

When We Die Do We Just Go Poof?

Dear Bonnie: I really need to know that there is life after death and that we don't just go 'poof' and we're gone. Can you elaborate for me? – Danielle

Dear Danielle: I can assure you that we don't just go 'poof' and there is more to this life than just an ending. I know it can be hard to grasp the concept when your faith has been challenged and you are feeling alone, but please know that your loved ones are very much alive in the spirit world.

I feel that everyone should experience seeing a connection to the other side so that they will know that life goes on and love never dies. This is what a medium does, especially during an event. We show you how the link can happen in a large gathering. If you are interested but have a fear of having a private reading, an event is the place to go and watch a medium work.

Everyone has a different style of presenting the spirit world to his or her audience, and you might connect to one medium more than another. I know I have my favorites who I like to watch and how they present the spirit world. I always tell my clients that I am the gentlest medium you can find. It's more like sitting down with a friend and having a cup of tea.

I named my television show on Leominster Access Television "The Medium Next Door" because I wanted to take away the fear of having a reading and replace it with, "Wow, what a blessing that was!"

A medium is meant to be the conduit, or middleman, who can bring your loved one to you for a conversation that you need and want. What could be more precious than that? The experience of hearing from your loved ones is priceless to many.

A medium's job is to give you evidence that your loved ones are still here with you and to convey the message of love that we all miss from them not being here physically. We can give you proof that they know about the amazing moments we have had since they left us.

Our loved ones will also send us signs, like songs on the radio, the scent of our grandmother's perfume, a knocking sound, or the appearance of a cardinal, to let us know they are near and watching out for us.

I like to bring in some lightheartedness when I give readings to ease the fear people may have, while at the same time showing compassion and giving evidential proof so there is no doubt of who is coming through for you during a reading.

In the end, it's all in how you want to perceive the experience. For myself, it's a blessing every time I bring a loved one close enough that you can almost feel them so that you will know they didn't just go 'poof' and disappear forever. They are always with you.

Dreamtime

I absolutely do believe in Heaven, and as a medium, I can assure you it does exist. I know that's easy for me to say since I work with spirit and Heaven every day. As a medium who does this work for healing purposes, I see a lot of hurt in the world and certain circumstances that happen for which there are no answers. I can only tell you what I have been shown and heard from the spirit world.

Early at the beginning of opening up to spirit and using my gifts, spirit would show me in my dream time how beautiful Heaven is. I would come into consciousness and be brought to a beautiful field with flowers and grass, skies so blue, colors so much more vivid and bright. I was shown all the animals walking together in pastures that had no fences, animals that here on Earth would be natural enemies, but in Heaven were nothing less than loving.

One night, I sat straight up in bed with amazement as they let me hear the music that was being played in Heaven, so much more magical than you could imagine. It sounds like a fairy tale, for sure. I feel I am no more special than anyone else, but I am here to teach the things I see and hear so others will know for certain that Heaven does exist.

I sometimes now wake to see and listen to myself having complete conversations with those I love on the other side. I don't always remember what we were saying, but I do get to see a little of what's taking place. One night, I even woke up knowing I was in Heaven, having a conversation with my mom.

In Heaven, there are many levels of enlightenment. For example, if you have learned your life lessons and your soul has grown and expanded, you would start at a higher level than someone who has made bad choices for themselves and others. They would start their journey in Heaven at a lower level until more light could be brought to them. Light always takes precedence over dark, just like good always conquers evil.

We are all God's children, and He doesn't want to punish us. He wants us to become the most loving version of ourselves that we can be. Earth is our schoolroom, where the lessons are learned. We will never live a life without obstacles to overcome or hard decisions to be made. They are the lessons we need to go through and learn from, allowing our souls the opportunity to learn unconditional love for others and ourselves.

Your life is all about making choices. Choose wisely for yourself, and Earth might seem a little more like Heaven.

Bad Spirits in Heaven? Well, then it Wouldn't be Heaven

Dear Bonnie: Do you believe there is a bad place or bad spirits in heaven? You always talk about the good stuff, but I am wondering is that because you leave the rest out. — Bruce

Dear Bruce: Indeed, I would much rather talk about light and love rather than the dark, which there surely is.

When I was a little girl, my mom, who was very spiritual, used to look at me when I was not so nice and maybe a little cranky. She would tell me, "There is an angel on your left shoulder and the devil on your right shoulder, and you had better knock him off." She would watch me as I laughed, which took away the crankiness, and pretend to knock the devil off my right shoulder.

You see, there is always a choice when it comes to every decision we make in life. Being a medium, I choose to do my work only in the white light of God. I have seen things in the spirit world that have scared the pants off me, but knowing in my heart that good always outweighs the bad, I know the second I think of God they go 'poof'. Truly, anything that was there disappears.

I believe that as souls living in this lifetime, we all have choices in our lives that are made from love or fear. It's that basic. There is always a good choice or a bad direction. There are, and always will be, two sides to every coin: love vs. fear, angel vs. devil, trust vs. worry, glory vs. shame, truth vs. falsehood, and light vs. darkness. The choice is yours.

We all have God's free will, and that means no one can make our decisions for us. In the spiritual world, they can shine a light to show us the way, they can manipulate changes so that we may see, but in the end, it's all on us and the choices we make.

Everyone will face choices they need to make that will push boundaries in their beliefs at one time or another, but if you have love, trust, and truth in your heart, the choices get easier to make.

Are there bad spirits in Heaven? No, or it wouldn't be Heaven. That doesn't mean they don't exist. I do believe there are different levels of Heaven, meaning someone very enlightened who has lived many soul lives might start at a higher level than someone who still needs to grow.

Bad spirits don't want to hang out with people who are of the light. It's like a teetotaler might never want to go hang out in a bar. At the end of the day, it's about making a choice. Do I want to hang out with the good guys or take a chance getting to know the bad guys? For me, that's a no to the latter.

There will always be good vs. evil, and it will always be your choice. Make each decision in your life by asking the question, "Will this bring me to the light where I may find peace?" If it does, go with that decision.

Remember my mom's analogy. The angel is on your left shoulder, the devil is on your right. Which one do you want to knock off? I sure do love my angels.

You are Creating Your Own Heaven

Dear Bonnie: What do you think Heaven looks like, and do our loved ones watch over us? — Brooke

Dear Brooke: I was giving a reading last week to a woman who came in asking to speak with her father. The reading started the way it usually does, with me giving evidence that her dad had come to speak with her. I always give a description of the person in Heaven that is before me. As I tune into the person's energy field in Heaven I feel if they are joyful or maybe a little stoic. Whatever their personality was here, it still is very much intact on the other side.

When my client's dad started to show me a boat on a lake surrounded by water and trees and a small cabin, I described in detail what I was seeing. The daughter said, "That's beautiful. We used to rent a cabin on a lake every summer while Dad was alive."

As I continued to talk to her dad, he said, "This is my version of Heaven. I need her to know this is my reality and what I surround myself with every day."

You see, her dad loved being at the lake on vacation with his family but, unfortunately, one week a year was all the time he had on Earth to enjoy himself with his family the way he wanted to. Now in Heaven, he surrounded himself with memories of these times and how much he cherished them.

He did have a regret of not spending more time with his family and saw that his idea of being a good husband and father was providing for them so they would never be without the things he thought they needed. On the higher side of life, he saw things from a different perspective and wanted his daughter to know he wished he had spent more time with her and his family.

As his daughter began to weep gently, he assured her he was there now, watching her family grow and not missing out on any family events, giving me proof of birthdays, weddings and even showing me how he was talking to and keeping her little daughter, his granddaughter, company by playing tea with her as she sat on her little pink table and chairs.

"Oh!" she said. "That's who she has been talking to!"

I informed her that her dad was very much still in their lives, leaving her with the message of making sure everyone made the effort in the family to go to the get-togethers, as these are the most important times in our lives. "Make memories," he told his daughter. "The rest will follow."

Cherished times and memories cannot be taken away and will continue with you creating your version of Heaven. Enjoy your life now and create a beautiful Heaven while you're at it. Love is the most important thing in life.

The Transition into Heaven

I once was driving my car home one night, and the snow started to swirl around me. It was peaceful and sparking, and I heard a voice from a spirit telling me this feeling I was having and the beauty I was seeing was what surrounds us as we transition into Heaven. The feeling was one of tranquility. People who have had near-death experiences often say they saw or felt surrounded by a vibrant white, shimmering, light, sometimes appearing as a tunnel.

After years of talking to your loved ones who are in Heaven, I am always amazed when they begin to tell me their version of Heaven. What does that mean? Each one of us will be able to manifest our version of Heaven. Whatever you can think of you can energetically manifest your surroundings in Heaven.

My version of being in Heaven might be totally different from your version. So, with that being said, when I see my mom in Heaven, as we do visit Heaven at night in our dream time, I will see her in the log cabin my dad built for her on a peaceful lake. She is entertaining her family as she always did here on Earth. That is her version of Heaven.

When I see my dad, who was a horse breeder and trainer here on Earth, I always see him with his favorite horses, riding around either using a saddle or using the jogging cart that he used to train horses with.

Your Heaven is going to look to you what you can most imagine for yourself. When I am giving a reading to a loved one, I often ask the person in Heaven to show me their version of it. Believe me, they are very different versions of Heaven.

Some loved ones show me they are skiing at the top of a beautiful mountain or golfing on the most beautiful golf course you have ever seen. Some tell me the music is amazing and they go to all the concerts. Others want their loved ones who are here on Earth to know that Heaven is for real, and they see Jesus and the angels and are right beside them, often telling their loved ones to have faith.

We are making our own version of Heaven as we go through our lives. What we love to do here we can do when we transform to the higher side of life. You are creating your Heaven now. If you like the beach, go to the beach and create what you love now. Heaven is right beside us. It is simply a dimension invisible to most eyes. Consciousness is never lost; it is just transformed. Your reality on earth can be whatever you choose to manifest, and your Heaven can be just as real.

Children in Heaven

Dear Bonnie: Do you see children in Heaven? I have a child in Heaven and wonder if she is okay every day. — Taylor

Dear Taylor: Yes, I do see children in heaven, and I am sorry for your loss. I believe losing a child is one of the hardest things we can go through in life.

I would like to share with you one of the first times I ever saw a child in Heaven. I was at the Omega Institute in Rhinebeck, N.Y., training at the International Mediumship Week with some of the world's top mediums. James Van Praagh and John Holland were two of my teachers.

This was my first training where I had to go and spend the week. Every day we were shown different ways to bring through spirit. On this particular day, Van Praagh had us all pair up with another medium. There were 100 of us there. I was matched up with a nice woman who was a little bit older than me and who'd had more training than I had at that time.

This turned out to be a blessing because Judy was a wonderful help. Van Praagh asked us to give each other the name, age, and relationship of someone we wanted to bring through from the other side. Judy looked at me and said, "Ben, he is my nephew and Godson, and he is five years old." I looked at Judy with a little trepidation and told her I had never brought a child through or asked a child to come through to me before. She said, "That is why spirit put you with me."

I did not know how I felt about asking a child in heaven to join me, but as I closed my eyes for a moment, I saw Ben. I was seeing the smallest littlest boy I had ever seen appear. Ben looked more like a three-year-old, not the five-year-old Judy had given me. She explained that Ben had cancer and had not grown at the same rate as other children his age.

Yet here he appeared before me happy and healthy-looking. He came through with vitality and full clarity. I could easily hear him as he was speaking to me. He talked and answered my questions just as any five-year-old would. I could see him standing before me in his little jeans and his turtleneck shirt, his dark hair cut with his bangs going straight across his forehead. He was adorable.

Ben and I began to have a conversation. "Ben, do you visit your mom?"

"Oh yes," he exclaimed with joy. "I play all around her feet with my truck." Ben showed me in my mind his mother at the kitchen stove cooking. I told him, "I am here with your Aunt Judy," and with his eyes full of expression he answered, "I like Aunt Judy." But then his face softened, and he told me "I miss mommy!!," which kind of took my breath away.

Trying my best to go on, Judy told me to ask him about his cat. "Yes, I see my cat. My cat likes to be patted just like this, down the back and up the tail." Ben showed me the motions, doing this twice in a row. I looked at Judy and gave her his answer. "Yes, that is exactly how Ben pets his cat." "Ben, do you play all the time?" "I play a lot," he answered with a grin, "But I learn, too," showing me there was school in Heaven.

I could have stayed there talking and interviewing Ben all day, but our time was up, and I had to say goodbye. I thanked Ben for coming to talk to me. The session ended, but before I left him, I told Ben I loved him. Ben didn't want to leave. He wanted to stay chatting with me. I finally had to tell him I had to go but encouraged him to go and play with his truck as he had shown me earlier. He did just that with an adorable smile on his face.

This new experience made me both sad and happy at the same time, knowing that Ben was very much alive and doing well in Heaven, but still missing his mommy here on Earth, even though he was still very much around her and his favorite cat. I have had many children now come to talk to me, even wanting to show me around. I know in all my heart that they are cared for and loved by many in the spirit world. They grow at a slower pace but do grow up to help others, even caring for the children that come after them and helping them to adjust to making Heaven their home.

If you feel the presence of a child around you, there probably is one. Welcome them with an open heart because, like Ben, they can hear you. Ben visited me a few times after coming home from school that week. I think he knew I was a little sad and that he could cheer me up with his beautiful smile. Talk to them, embrace them, and know they are there with you always and they are okay.

Talking to Heaven

Dear Bonnie: I am in so much pain after the loss of my loved one. Is my suffering keeping my loved one 'away' from me? Is it possible that I'm blocking communication? — Mary

Dear Mary: When a loved one passes, we can be feeling so much pain that we may indeed be blocking our loved one from visiting us in dreams or even sending signs at first. It takes a lot of energy for spirit to come through or to send signs since we are all energy. Sometimes when a soul passes and is in Heaven it can take a while for that loved one to regain his or her energy to enable them to come through.

If your loved one was sick for a long period, they may be taking that time in Heaven to regain the energy that was lost due to being sick. The other side of the scenario could be that you are in distress with their passing, and they don't want to add to the sadness you are already feeling.

There are times when souls patiently wait for the right moment to come through when they believe you will be able to hear from them without causing too much pain or grief to you.

Could you be missing the signs that your loved ones are near? Many times, especially at night, we have visits with those whom we love but never remember them. Before going to bed at night, take a moment after saying your prayers to ask that you remember the visit clearly when you wake up. I know that we all visit Heaven at night in our dream state. Some of us remember and others do not.

Some other signs that you could be missing are gentle breezes or the feeling of someone softly rubbing your arm, letting you know they are around you. A special song that suddenly comes on while you're listening to the radio can bring their memory alive. Try to listen for the subtle noises or the feelings that surround you during the day. A hug from Heaven may feel a little like that feeling of bliss that everything will be okay, almost like an angel wrapping his wings around you in protection. When you're ready, a sign will appear in a form that you can understand.

Your loved ones want nothing more than to reach out to you, letting you know that they are okay, and want only for you to know they are safe and at peace. Give the conversation some time, for time stands still in Heaven, so what may appear to be forever to you is but a fraction of a second to your loved one.

When the two worlds are ready for the communication to begin, there will be no stopping your loved one from coming through for you.

TIPS ON COMMUNICATING WITH YOUR LOVED ONES

1. Be open to receiving. Many times during a reading, loved ones in heaven will tell me how they are trying to reach out and start the communication or ways that they are coming through to give you a sign. When I tell clients what to look for, many have already been seeing the signs and not understanding it was from spirit. Sometimes signs can seem like a coincidence.
2. Pay attention to what's happening around you. Are the lights flashing in the room you're in or are the dogs barking or wagging their tails back and forth for no apparent reason or explanation? Animals often see spirit and can see who is coming to visit you.
3. Notice what your children are saying or doing. If you see your children having a conversation with someone who's not there, it's more than likely that their grandparents are stopping in and keeping a helpful eye on them. Grandparents are very invested in knowing their grandchildren, even if they were not born before their passing.
4. Don't be stressed. Try to give your loved ones in Heaven the time they need to come through. In the meantime, try to hold them close in your heart and acknowledge their lives by speaking about them often and honoring the lives they lived while here on Earth. They love it when their memory is kept alive! And when the messages do start to flow, be sure to let them know you are receiving them, so it truly is a conversation from heaven. Let the conversation from heaven truly be a blessing.

Watch for the Signs

Dear Bonnie: Recently I lost someone very dear to me, a friend I have had since childhood. We didn't need to be together every day to know what the other one was thinking. We just knew when we needed to reach out and make a phone call. She became ill very fast and in two months she was gone. When her last days were near, I went to visit her in the hospital, where we agreed that we would always be in touch, and she promised to send me a sign. It's been almost six months, and I haven't felt her presence or received any signs. Am I missing something? It's unlike her to not keep a promise. Thanks, Rebecca

Dear Rebecca: Sometimes, when someone is still in the heavy grieving stage, we can miss the subtle signs that our loved ones can send. Signs from the spirit world are not always huge signs. They might be happening but are easy to miss if we are not aware of the ways our loved ones can reach out to us. I know your friend would not break that promise as well, so I am going to list some ways she might be trying to get in touch with you.

You might not be remembering or picking up the language of the spirit world and their new way of communicating. Please keep this list close by, and when you become more aware of the many ways she can reach out to you, you might just see that you have indeed seen a sign or two.

1. Dreams are the number one way we can receive a sign. When we are deep in sleep and the veil becomes thinner around three in the morning, we can receive a visit. A visit will seem more real than a dream. You might see what they are wearing or become aware that you are having a conversation with them. It happens more often than we might think. The key here is to set the intention to remember your visit.
2. Have you been seeing quick flashes of light or sparkles when you close your eyes or catch a glimpse of light flashing out of the corners of your eyes? Truly a sign your loved ones are near, and let's not forget the balls of white light you catch on your phone or pictures called orbs. We are all energy, and sometimes this is an easy way for your loved ones to appear or show up at a celebration.

3. Your loved ones can connect to you by sending you a thought or memory. Have you had a moment where you recall a time of being together and you didn't know where that thought was coming from? It could be your loved one reaching out to you.
4. Have you noticed when the lyrics of a song make you cry? Often, loved ones reach out through lyrics in a song. Pay attention. Those lyrics have a whole message inside of them for you.
5. Repetitive sounds or chimes. The spirit world can use that energy within them to make the clock ding or become louder, or the refrigerator can start making noises when you are nearby. There can be three knocks at the door and nobody there. It's their way of letting you know they are close by.
6. Feelings and tingles that pop up on your body like goosebumps. Have you ever just felt so loved for a moment that it takes your breath away? A hug from Heaven can do that. A breeze might appear out of nowhere, or a change in the temperature can be a sign as well that your loved one is right next to you.
7. Another way your loved one can reach you is through children and animals. Children, up until school age, and animals often see the spirit world, so your loved ones can come near and ask them to give you a hug or stare into your eyes to send you a sign of love. They know when you need that hug.
8. You might be finding coins and seeing cardinals or their favorite birds around you.
9. The television gets full of static when you walk into the room.
10. It might just be a faint whisper that you hardly notice that says, "I love you."

These are some of the ways your loved one can reach out, and you might not be aware. Give your loved ones some time to send a sign, because I know they are always trying to give you confirmation that they are near and at peace.

Spirit Animals Let You Know Loved Ones Are Still Nearby

Dear Bonnie: Since my father passed a few months ago, I keep seeing black crows and blackbirds everywhere. Could this be a sign my dad is sending? – Ivan

Dear Ivan: There are a couple of reasons these birds seem to be following you at this time. Did your dad have an association with these two types of birds? One possible scenario might be that your dad knows that when you see these particular birds, it makes you think of him. He might be sending these birds as a reminder that he is always around you and wants to make sure you know he is never far away.

When loved ones pass, their main concern for us is to let us know that even in death, they are still alive, and their soul is still with us. They want you to feel comforted at this time. They work their hardest at getting a sign to you at the moments you most need them.

If seeing these two birds makes you think of your father, then he is getting his message across: "I am fine, I have not left you."

The second scenario is that these birds are two of your spirit animals, guides that know you need to see and understand the power they have as they guide you. We have many guides throughout our lifetime, and many of them will change as our lives evolve and we need help with different areas.

We have one main guide who is with us from birth to the end of our Earthly journey and will escort us home to Heaven one day. But we may have many guides and angels that step into our lives when we are faced with challenges, especially the hard parts of our lives, when we may need a little extra help.

Spirit animals are also guides who provide extra strength and guidance during our lifetime. I have seen many spirit animal guides, many in my dream time, who will show up and offer support. If your spirit animals appear to you, it is for a reason. So, remembering to ask that spirit animal to reveal itself to you in your dream time or in meditation and asking, "How are you guiding me?" is crucial to finding out the answer.

I looked up the two birds that are appearing to you in a book called "Spirit Animals" by Dr. Steven Farmer. This book is a handy pocket guide. As your spirit animals appear you can look up their meanings. Please remember to use your intuition when asking them, "Why have you come?"

Crow: You're on the verge of manifesting something you have been working on for a while. Be very watchful over the next couple of days for any clear omens or signs that will guide you or teach you. Expect a big change soon. You've noticed something that's out of balance or an injustice that hasn't been addressed, and it is important to speak up about it. You're about to get a glimpse into some future event that affects you directly.

Blackbird: Let go of all your inhibitions and sing without concern for how it sounds or fear of others' disapproval. Archangel Uriel is with you, watching out for you and helping you connect with nature and nature spirits. Sound healing is one of your best treatments for whatever physical or emotional ailments or maladies you're experiencing.

Ivan, these are your two spirit guides at this moment. They change when our needs change. Your dad might very well be sending these two guides at this time to offer healing and insight that you have been in need of since his passing. These two guides seem to offer insight into healing as well as inspiration for the future.

Connecting with nature at this time is something important for you. Your dad is on the job, even sending an angel to watch over you. Take the time you need to heal but know in your heart that your dad is still just a thought away.

Orbs — Unexplained Lights from the Spirit World

Dear Bonnie: Sometimes I see lights, not a reflection of the sun or lights from an electrical source. They can look like free-floating balls of light. I have seen them flow into a room in which I am standing. Sometimes the lights flash. Once I saw a bright red light in front of me. Is there a spiritual significance to these lights? — Lois

Dear Lois: These free-floating lights are often referred to as orbs. Orbs are transparent balls or globes of light energy connected to spirits. Orbs are commonly found in photos but can be seen also with the naked eye, particularly around people or in highly energetic areas.

These orbs can be a variety of shapes, sizes, and colors. The colors of orbs can mean different things to different people. Overall, I've seen that the colors of an orb seem to coincide with the energy system in the body called the chakras. Bright, pure orb colors indicate beautiful energy coming forth.

For your particular case, Lois, the red color in the orb you saw was your grandfather. It was a strong and protective energy, like a great big hug for you. He watches over you from heaven. The white orbs were from your parents: the energy was meant to be encouraging and inspiring. Your parents want to communicate that you're on the right track in life and to stay the course.

Usually, when I give a reading, the client's loved ones who are in spirit tell me they have joined them during a celebration or major life event, such as a wedding or family gathering. I find this applies to every one of us. Just as the loved one was with you physically for all of the important occasions when they were alive, so they join you again for those events, only this time, they are present in spirit. This is why it is so very common to see orbs in wedding photos, graduation pictures, or family reunion snapshots.

Orbs are known as "spirit orbs." Just as orbs are energy, so are we, and so is spirit. Everything that surrounds us is energy and vibrates at an energetic frequency. Actions that raise our vibrational energy, and therefore make us more likely to experience orbs, include any spiritual ritual, such as prayer, worship, or healing service, such as Reiki. You may also see them while out in nature, which is highly spiritual and places you in a meditative mood, so you are more likely to observe orbs.

Pets, one of my favorite subjects, can easily experience orbs. Cats are particularly adept at seeing orbs. If your dog is wagging his tail or barking at "nothing," he's probably sensing spirit. Orbs have even been known to play with our pets, too. Maybe that's why cats love laser pointers so much.

Some people believe they can see faces inside the orbs. Orbs have been captured with distinctive facial features and even multiple faces in one orb.

As part of my research for this question, I asked my Facebook friends to share their stories and pictures of orbs. They flowed in with abundance. Thanks to all who participated.

Remember, spirits are incredibly creative and persistent in speaking with you. Your loved ones who have passed on will use every energetic tool at their disposal to reach out to you. Dreams, coins, synchronicities, and repeated sequences of the same number are some of the methods we've previously covered. Orbs, or light energy, are yet another amazing communication option.

When my father was four his mother passed away. At night he would see beautiful flashes and balls of white light above his bed. He found them particularly soothing when he was afraid. Whether these orbs were his mother's energy or a guardian angel, the result was the same: He felt peaceful and loved. When you see these flashes or orbs yourself, know that someone in heaven wants to share a sliver of their divine, eternal love with you, too.

Seeing My Mom and Dad in an Orb

Don't worry about that orb. It's likely a spirit.

Dear Bonnie: I know you have talked about orbs in one of your columns, but I would like to ask you about different-colored orbs and their meanings. I took a picture recently, and there was a pink orb next to my daughter. It kind of freaked me out. Do I have any need to worry about her? — Jade

Dear Jade: Let me tell you a little more about orbs. An orb is a spiritual vehicle for a loved one, angel or guide, or spiritual being to move them from one realm to another. Most orbs are pure white. Most people see orbs in pictures and not with their physical eyes. Animals also can see orbs because they can also see the spiritual world.

Of course, we have dominance over the spiritual world, so there is no need to be afraid. Truly, orbs are usually here to help us in some way or to bring us a message.

After that first column I wrote about orbs, people from all around the world started to send me photos and videos of orbs. One day, I was walking through my home while reading an email on my phone, and in my head, I was thinking orbs, orbs, orbs, and in the corner of the room, way up by the ceiling, I saw two white round lights. As I looked on, those white lights started to move down toward me.

I gasped a little, and as I did, each orb broke open, and there were the faces of my mother and father, looking younger than when they passed, and they each had a big smile on their face. I know they were saying, "See? Orbs are for real."

So, I did some more research and found out that the colors of the orbs usually coincide with the colors of the rainbow, like the colors of our energy system called the chakras. This makes sense to me since we are all energy.

Just last week, I took a picture of a photo of my father and me that was hanging on the wall, and I posted it to Facebook. Soon after, people asked me about the round pink ball held tightly in my arms and asked if it was in the original picture. When I went to look at the picture I had posted, I saw the pink ball, and when I enlarged the picture, it showed me a small white poodle all snuggled up under my arm. That poodle was my mom's poodle here on Earth.

So now I have seen a few colored orbs with spirits inside. I have not seen a dark-colored orb, but as I did my research online, I found that dark color to be the color of the root chakra, which is more earthy, so just another meaning and nothing to be afraid of.

So, remember, if you are ever fearful of anything spiritual, say a prayer to God and the angels and ask whatever it is to go away. But if you're curious like me, ask the orb who they are and what message they are bringing to you, because if it is from Heaven, it's a great message of love and hope.

I hope this answers more of your questions on orbs. If you see those bright white balls of lights in your pictures that you have taken during a wedding or birthday celebration, your loved ones want to let you know that when you are celebrating, they are right beside you.

Orbs Galore

Seeing orbs in photos? They're spirits of loved ones.

So many readers have been asking about orbs and sending me pictures and videos asking me to view them.

Have you ever taken a picture, and when you go back to look at it, there is a ball of light or a faint image of a person? The light might have been shaped like a ball or another shape or even a different color.

What is an orb? Why are these balls of energy in my photos? So many questions, and where do you turn? I hope this sheds some light on the subject, (no pun intended).

An orb is a transparent ball of light energy that is connected to spirits. Orbs can be spotted in photos or even videos. People have written to me saying their security cameras are catching these balls of light. It's intriguing that many people would like an explanation and a confirmation that it is something. Some are even asking if they need to be worried.

Lots of times when I am giving a reading, a loved one in spirit will say, "Tell them to look closely at their wedding photo. They will see a ball of light. That is me." Your loved ones are still attending the ceremonies that mean so much to you.

During these trying times that we are having worldwide, the spirit world is so active because they really want you to know that your loved ones in heaven are close by, offering protection and love during these trying times. It is like they are showing up big-time to provide their support.

Even though a soul cannot be here in the physical form, it is still very much around you and your loved ones. People want validation that this is their loved one coming through in the picture. I often tell people to look at the picture, close their eyes and try to make a connection on their own. If you get a feeling or sense your father's presence, for instance, while looking at the picture, or you can hear his voice inside your head, you just need to trust your instincts.

Some mediums can see inside the orb or give you a description of who is around you in these energy balls of light. When I started to receive so many requests, I said out loud to the spirit world, "What is up with all these questions about orbs?" Just like magic, two orbs appeared from the top of my ceiling and started to make their way down to me, and as they did, they burst open one at a time.

One was the face of my mother and the next was the face of my father. I could tell they were trying to tell me that there was no denying these balls of light. They looked so happy! I know they are still teaching me from the other side, as they did when they were here. Even though I am a medium, it still was magnificent to see. I offered up thanks to Mom and Dad.

So, you see, I can say with certainty that we are all energy, and energy can never be taken away; it only transcends. These balls of lights can be different shapes and colors, and maybe that is because we are all not alike here in the physical as well.

If you have a picture or a video with flashes or balls of light, and you feel like you need a professional opinion, please make an appointment with a medium. Just like we sometimes need a doctor or a dentist, a medium is a profession as well, and it might take a little time to tune in to the spirit world and get the answers you are looking for.

I do have a video that I created that can be found on my website, www.bonniepagemedium.com. If you have more questions, please watch it.

Your loved ones are still with you from up above, watching and caring from a place of love, and are very much always with you. Look for the signs.

Signs are Everywhere, even in a Fortune Cookie

Dear Bonnie: I try to stay focused on a spiritual path, but sometimes I seem to slip off and find my ego calling the shots. It's hard to be spiritual when something happens for a colleague that you have been trying to succeed at, and it's not happening for you. I find myself jealous, and resentment slips in, and I know that is not being very spiritual. What should I do? — Martha

Dear Martha: Last week in my center, I was giving a reading to a woman who was getting a message from her dad in Heaven. He kept giving me pictures of horses and then showed me a saddle and some ribbons: red, to be exact. It turns out he was an avid rider and had been in many horse shows and won many ribbons.

After the reading was complete, we continued to talk about how her dad had raised horses to show at events. My dad also had raised and raced Standardbred racehorses. We continued talking about standard breeds and thoroughbreds and the difference between the two, how our dads had so much in common, and the bond between our dads and ourselves.

That night, my son called me as I was leaving work and asked if my husband and I would join him at a Chinese restaurant we love. We had an amazing meal, and at the end, the server brought our fortune cookies. I opened mine and started to laugh as I read the words: "Anyone can 'start,' only the thoroughbred will 'finish'!"

I took that little fortune, slipped it into my pocket, and brought it home, knowing it not only had a more significant meaning but also that my dad had been at and heard the reading I had given that same day. If I weren't amazed enough, I felt something inside of me saying that this is going to mean more to you. I took that little piece of paper home and pinned it up on a mirror, telling my dad in my mind, "Okay. I am listening and I received your sign."

It didn't end there, though. Two days later I would need these words of encouragement as I got the news that some goals I have been trying to achieve would take a little longer than I had expected. Walking around my home, feeling disappointed for myself, I heard a little voice inside my head say, "Go look at your fortune. Anyone can 'start,' only the thoroughbred will 'finish!'"

Oh my, not only did these words have the encouragement I needed to hear, but also left me with the message, "We are here in spirit supporting you. Things might not be happening as fast as you would like but keep going ahead and someday you will be at the finish line. A steady pace is what will get you to the finish line. Spirit knows all, not only about the future but also how to get you there."

If you look for the signs, they are there, even in a cookie. Words and signs from Heaven are all around you. Don't give up. Be the one who finishes what you started. God always tells me, "Put on your blinders; straight ahead and don't let your earthly feelings get the best of you."

You are loved, and no one wants you to achieve your goals more than everyone in heaven. Listen as they cheer you on.

Loved Ones Send Signs — It's Up to Us to Read Them

I believe that when someone passes, the first thing they want to do is send us a sign to let us know they have arrived at their destination, Heaven. It's like when you were a teenager and your mom and dad started to let you go out with your friends. They wanted to make sure you were safe and sound, so you needed to call and check in occasionally. Our loved ones do not want us to have a worry or be left with the thought that they have died and it's the end of them being in our lives. It's very much the opposite. They now have the ability to see, hear, and know what is going on with us.

Souls that pass have the choice of going into the white light, where their loved ones are waiting or, if they choose, they can take their time to check in on family members and friends before they transition to their Heavenly home. We have God's free will. It is their choice. Sooner more often than later they will see that white light and someone patiently waiting for them, and the transition will happen.

Before my dad passed, I was in my dream time, and in the energy space where spirit can show you many things, I came to realize I was being shown a room where all of my dad's family were waiting for him. His mother had passed when he was just four, and I had only seen pictures of her. I have one particular picture of her and my grandfather together sitting on my hutch in my dining room.

When I recognized her, she stood up from where she was sitting with the rest of the family and began to wave frantically to me as she knew I could see her. She looked exactly like she did in my picture, showing me her beautiful smile as she was so happy to acknowledge that we were seeing each other and having a connection. It was a happy moment, but I began to realize that what I was seeing was my dad's family preparing for him and waiting to greet him when he arrived. I was both happy and sad.

Two days later, after my dad went to be in Heaven, I was sitting in the living room. I became aware of the smell of smoke around me. I jumped up out of my chair to see if anything was burning. One of the psychic gifts is called clairolfactory, or clear smell. It's just one way of receiving a message. Someone might be able to smell a grandmother's perfume or a father's aftershave. It's associated with a spirit person.

So, after checking my house to see if there was a fire and realizing nothing was burning, I sat back in my chair, and the smell of smoke came back again, stronger this time. It took me a moment to realize that it was my dad's message to me: The smoke represented the wood stove my dad kept constantly going in his home. He loved the wood-burning stove in his kitchen. He loved the warmth and feeling of contentment that it brought into his life.

As soon as I caught on, I smiled to myself and said out loud. "Dad, I know it's you. Thank you for the sign. I know you're safe and sound." I was still sad but happy to know he was with his mom and family who he had longed to see.

There are many signs, and usually they mean something to both you and your loved one who has passed. They are a way of sharing a memory, bringing comfort to those who are left behind in the physical world.

Other signs may come from your ability to "clear-taste." This ability is called clairgustance, the ability to psychically taste a substance, liquid, or food without actually putting anything in your mouth. You might be able to taste your loved one's favorite food or a cigarette or pipe they smoked.

Stay aware of the things going on around you after the passing of a loved one or when you feel sad. Everyone in heaven knows our thoughts and will try to communicate one way or another.

Like I always say, love never dies, and your loved ones are always connected to you, just in a different way but always from the heart. When you receive a sign, acknowledge it, and give thanks to the spirit you feel is sending the sign. It is just a new way to keep the conversation and relationship alive until we meet again.

More Signs

Hearing knocks? Seeing Shadows? Your passed loved ones are trying to help.

Dear Bonnie: I need some help. I have been having a tough time lately. The other day I was trying to sleep, and I kept hearing noises, but nobody was there. I sat up and thought I saw a shadow. However, the next day I went on a walk to the park, and it was getting dark, and when I looked up at the trees moving in the wind, I felt an overwhelming presence of happiness fill my body. Today I was listening to music, and I heard a knock on the door and there was no one there. What does this all mean? Please help me to understand. – Rhianna

Dear Rhianna: I am sorry you are going through tough times lately, but do not feel alone. I believe that is what your loved ones in Heaven are trying to tell you as well.

When we are troubled about the things that are happening around us, our loved ones gather near to let us know they are close and are giving us support. The knock on the door has been heard by many, including me. I love it when it happens because it makes you answer the door, and when you open the door, no one is there. It is a clear sign that they are sending to let you know they are with you.

The fact that you're seeing shadows and hearing noises tells me they are trying to get that message to you loud and clear. When you were taking that walk, and you glanced up and saw the trees moving with the wind and you felt total peace, that was them comforting you.

My mom came through to me after she passed and told me she could shine a light on a difficult situation but not change the situation. I know our loved ones are with us each day, and they know our troubles as well as our celebrations. The way they send comfort is in these little signs. Keep watching for them, say thank you to them for watching over you, and know you are never alone in good times and in troubled times.

Cardinals are God's Messengers

Dear Bonnie: I was having a reading with you when you mentioned that my dad and mom were sending me cardinals to represent themselves as a message from heaven that they were near. You gave details of exactly when the birds were visiting and how I was able to see them from my kitchen window. It kind of freaked me out as to how accurate your vision was. When I arrived at my house that afternoon, the male and female cardinal were sitting there next to the window you described earlier. Can you tell me a little bit more about the meaning of these two birds? — Carly

Dear Carly: We are often very connected to birds, and they are mentioned many times in the Bible as being messengers and seers for God. A seer is a person or creature that can see the future and deliver these messages.

The cardinal is believed to be a seer for the spiritual world, and this is symbolized by the crest on its head. The crest is thought to be a sign of importance, spiritual connections, and intelligence.

The word itself, "cardinal," comes from the Latin word cardo, which means "hinge." The cardinal is serving as the hinge on the doorway between Heaven and Earth. The cardinal is also known for its loud whistle, so getting your attention is much easier. This bird gains your attention and asks you to listen to your inner voice.

When a cardinal is trying to get your attention, I tell my clients to pay attention to the feeling you get as they draw near. Paying attention to your gut feeling will leave you with a sense of who in Heaven is trying to gain your attention. Close your eyes for a moment to feel what message your loved one is sending to you. It is just another way to receive a message yourself without the help of a medium or third party.

The cardinal represents togetherness, as they mate for life. They ask you to seek inner peace and know that you are absolutely loved. The spiritual message from your loved one in heaven is often one of love, guidance, and protection. They tell you to find a love that is yours forever and make sweet memories and connections that can never be broken.

All that God and those in Heaven wish is for you to find and experience unconditional love for yourself and others.

On a personal note, when my beloved dog, Sinbad, was passing, a cardinal flitted from window to window where I was sitting with him, keeping him company, as I knew he would be leaving soon. This cardinal gave me courage and strength, as I knew he was the messenger from spirit that day that neither myself nor Sinbad was alone.

Seeing 11:11? It's a Messenger from Heaven

I have been waking up to the alarm clock showing me the time of 11:11 on numerous occasions and wondered what it could mean. So, I did a little research. Keep in mind that the universe or God might be sending out these numbers as well, as loved ones who have passed, and they can have different meanings to different people.

It seems that these numbers, in particular, coincide with what's going on in your thoughts and life at the time they pop up.

I'll tell you a little about my story. One day recently, I had gone out and filled the bird feeders. I came back inside and was staring out the window watching the birds eat when a beautiful cardinal came. Now, I know they are a sign from Heaven, so I said, "Hello, Mom," and all of a sudden, a light that was not on turned on all by itself.

I am a medium, and these things still excite me but, being a little skeptical, I checked the connection and, sure enough, the plug had to be physically turned on for that to happen. It had not been.

I have a clock on my mantle that came from my mom that I inherited years ago that sits there just because it's pretty. It's an old-fashioned clock that you need to wind and set to get going, and I have never bothered to do any of that, though I do polish it now and then, (and even that I hadn't done in a while).

Well, I went to bed that evening and came into consciousness when I heard a voice telling me, "Something special is happening for you in Heaven, and we are going to play some music for you." I often hear voices in Heaven, so I just smiled, but I opened my eyes to look at the clock, and when I did, 11:11 appeared. And then, out of nowhere, my mom's clock in the living room started to chime.

But it didn't stop there.

The next night, after being asleep for two hours, I was awakened at the same time, 11:11, but this time my mom's clock was playing a tune! I wouldn't believe it if I hadn't seen or heard it myself, but I did and I was amazed. I called my sister, who explained that my mom often gets in touch with her in the same manner.

Here is what I found out about the numbers 11:11, but there are many different opinions out there on what these numbers mean. So, you might need to decide what they mean to you and where they fit into your life.

God or the universe may be trying to send you the message that your thoughts are manifesting in the now and to be careful what you let into your consciousness. You are a spiritual being having a human experience and are the creator of your own time here on Earth.

These numbers are often looked at as "angel numbers" that give validation that they are close by while watching and guiding you on the path you want to create for yourself.

This is the time to picture big, exciting thoughts about how you can live your life and how you can make a difference in the world for future generations. Angels are God's messengers, and they bring to you messages of hope to align you on your path.

When I first started to see the angels a few years ago, Archangel Metatron and his twin brother came to me with the message that God wanted me for something big, and soon after I started to share my gifts as a medium.

These numbers tell you your angels are saying, "Take action now, for it is your time to create the life you choose for yourself." Stay focused, and if you need to step away from the crowd or your friends for a time to stay in alignment with your purpose, it is okay to do so. Things are manifesting quickly, so be on your toes, expecting only the best for your life. Your dreams are coming to fruition.

Your loved ones in Heaven can also be telling you they are close by and watching your dreams as they come offering support and telling you not to be afraid.

Go for it. This is what you have worked hard to achieve. Keep watching and paying attention. It's your time to shine. Something special is happening in Heaven. Be ready for it.

You Are My Sunshine

Dear Bonnie: Have you experienced a sign from Heaven that is so clear it cannot be explained away?

Dear Susan: There are many signs from our loved ones in heaven that we receive every day. Some are clearer than others, but then some signs come to us in a manner that no one could possibly explain away.

Recently, at a class I was giving in my Healing and Learning Center, a group of students gathered. I began the class with a prayer asking spirit to join us. This class was about communicating with our loved ones and was meant for anyone who wished to learn how to receive a sign on their own. We started with a guided meditation that I created, and that I end many group events with, called "Love Never Dies".

After the meditation was over and many tears were shed, the group of students formed a circle and we started to work with cards that I made called "Messages from Heaven". Each of the 52 cards in this deck has a message that I received from working with spirit, and no two cards are alike.

I taught the class how to shuffle the deck while asking for a message from the loved one they wanted to communicate with while saying their name in their minds. Then I asked them to feel which card was meant for them and to take it out of the deck. Each student sat with a card facing down until everyone was done. We then proceeded to go around the circle, giving the name and relationship of the person on the other side that we wanted to hear from.

Cards are an amazing tool for receiving messages, and they actually, work very well. When it was time for my student named Tom to share what he had received he flipped over his card that read, "You are my sunshine." We all listened to Tom as he told us how his mom had always sung that song to him as a boy. Their bond with each other was very strong, and he missed her presence in his life every day.

When I tuned into her energy, she asked me to give him another message: She needed him to know that she still wanted everyone to enjoy the upcoming Easter holiday and began showing me a ham with all the fixings. When I spoke the words she was giving me, Tom explained that his mother had passed one year ago on Easter Day, but the signs didn't stop there.

When Tom got home that night, he received a picture from his daughter and her mom who were vacationing in Myrtle Beach together and had gotten tattoos that day. Tom sent me the picture of the card he had drawn in my class., "You are my sunshine," and the picture he received from his daughter showing their tattoos. The tattoos read on one of the feet, "You are my sunshine" and on the other of his daughter's feet, "My only sunshine".

Tom sent me both pictures together. All I could say was, "Amazing!" Not only did Tom's lovely mom get a message to her son, but she also let him know she was watching his family and keeping them all close together in her heart. She is no longer in the physical world, but very much alive and living life every day with those who she loves.

Is My Deceased Relative Trying to Contact Me?

Dear Bonnie: I feel that I am receiving signs from a relative who died. The signs are not spooky; in fact, I find them comforting. Am I imagining things, or are our loved ones who have died able to communicate with us? If so, how do they do it without voices or bodies? — Mary

Dear Mary: Great question! My experience shows that dreams, especially vivid, full-color dreams where you have complete conversations with the person who has passed, are the number one way our deceased loved ones communicate with us. Before you go to sleep, ask to speak with the deceased via your dreams. If you tend not to remember dreams, keep a pen and paper by your nightstand. As soon as you wake up, jot down the dream. The insights can be amazing!

Spirits are pure vibrational energy and can influence another person's thoughts, manipulate electrical currents and sound waves, and create "coincidences" around us. If dreams don't work for you, spirit will try another method to communicate with you. Some common other signs include:

- Feathers in places unlikely to have feathers, such as in a corporate office building.
- Birds, butterflies and ladybugs in unlikely places and times, like the middle of winter.
- Sound. Music that reminds you of that particular person that is not likely to be played on the radio or otherwise. Knocking (sounds like knocking on the front door) and no one is there.
- Electronics, TVs, phones, or even appliances that turn on/off without logical explanation.
- Pennies or coins in places where there are not likely to be coins, like on a nature hike. Look at the coin's date; it might be meaningful!
- Numbers in a specific sequence that is meaningful to you, seen repeatedly. As you're thinking of a loved one who has passed,

check out the time on a digital clock, license plates on the cars near you, or even the numbers as you're doing bills. You might be pleasantly surprised!

- The specific scent that accompanied that person in life, such as cigar smoke or a particular perfume that cannot be explained otherwise. Once I was sitting in my smoke-free, two-story home, thinking of my deceased grandfather, and suddenly the whole house smelled like the brand of cigar he used to smoke!

If, in life, that loved one had a special or unique way of communicating their love to you, look for that special sign. For example, I had a relative who loved flowers and gardening while he was alive. This winter, I was standing outside on my walkway, thinking of him, and looking out at the road, and a flower delivery truck drove by. To my surprise, the florist turned around and met me on my walkway instead!

He explained that my new neighbor, the flowers' intended recipient, was not home, and it was too cold to leave the flowers on their doorstep outside. The florist requested I "babysit" the flowers in my home until my neighbor returned. I had the pleasure of enjoying two dozen white roses all afternoon! I just know it was a nod from heaven.

Spiritual Communication

Dear Bonnie: My dad passed away six weeks ago, and I am devastated. Not only was he my rock and the person that really got me, but he was the only person on Earth I trusted completely. Do not get me wrong; I love my mom, but my dad always knew what I was thinking and why, and he never judged me and always made me feel safe.

So, here is the thing: I have been waking up every night now around 3 a.m. I will feel a presence and suddenly I'll jump up out of bed, and when I go to look at the clock the time has been all around that time. My question to you is, am I going crazy? Is this my dad trying to communicate with me and does he have a message for me? - Pearl

Dear Pearl: Our dads often are very special people in our lives. Remember, we pick our parents before we are born, so chances are that connection is one of the strongest in our lives. We often come down to Earth with our soul's family, so it is a very real chance you and your father have been through many lifetimes together. We often switch who will be who in relationships, but our soul's family sticks together. You are not crazy, feeling the presence of your dad when he comes to visit you during the night.

Often the hours around 3 a.m. seem to be the sacred hour of communication from the other side. Think of it in this way; your dad crosses over, and he knows how much you miss him and how you are grieving the loss of his physical presence. So, he tries to tell you he arrived safely at his destination and not to worry. It's almost like two parents that go on vacation, and they leave their kids with someone to watch over them while they are away. But they worry about them, and they know they will be missed, so they call the first chance they get.

The same happens when someone crosses over. Your loved ones want to let you know they have reached their destination and want to comfort you and let you know they will see you again one day. In the meantime, these visits are a way to communicate. The veil between the two worlds is thinner and more easily accessible around the hours of 3 a.m..., making communication more available to us.

I am living proof of this happening to me for years. It was almost like someone would shake me awake, and when I could not fall back asleep, I would get up and have a cup of tea. This was a normal thing for me, so much so that sometimes my husband would get up to find me sitting and having tea, and he would say, "They woke you up again?" I would reply "Yes, but it is okay." It's not such a bad thing knowing I had had a visit. In fact, it was comforting.

Her Husband is Letting Her Know He is Still with Her

Dear Bonnie: My husband of 30 years passed away with coronavirus. I am grieving for the person that was my rock. I loved him dearly and still cannot believe he is gone. When I go to bed at night, I turn off the light and look up at the ceiling and sometimes see flashes of little lights, sometimes red and orange. Sometimes there are exceedingly small images just like a photograph, and I have definitely recognized my husband and other people in them. They are gone in an instant, but I feel so calm and not at all frightened. I would love to hear what you make of this. — Monica

Dear Monica: All are signs from heaven. Please go with your gut feeling that these are signs from your husband. I believe he wants you to know he is very much around you even though it is not in the physical. We are all made up of energy, and he is working hard to let you know he is and always will be watching and caring for you.

I love how you can see the small pictures. When you can see the spirit world, it is the gift of clairvoyance. Clairvoyance is clear-seeing and is one of the many ways spirit uses to communicate with us. When we can see signs, pictures, loved ones' faces and objects, almost like little movies being played, spirit uses your gifts to see clearly. This is the spirit world using one or more of your psychic centers.

We all are born with psychic centers called chakras, and they can be opened after a loved one passes. It is one way they let us know there is so much more to life than we know. Your husband is showing you who he is within Heaven by sending the pictures of himself and who he is with, letting you know he is safe and not alone on his new journey. I am glad you are not frightened and feel comforted by what you are seeing.

Next time you see the lights and pictures, send out a thought. Simply ask, "What do you want me to know?" Close your eyes and wait for a sign or gut feeling of what your husband wants you to know. It is a new way of having a conversation with a loved one you are missing.

I always tell my clients that when a loved one passes to the higher side of life, they try so hard to get a message of love and reassurance that they are still with you, just in a different way. It is as if we left for vacation, and we wanted to let our family members know we made it to our destination. The first thing we would do is pick up the telephone to let them know we arrived safely.

Be on the lookout for other signs as well. Butterflies, ladybugs, cardinals, pennies, smelling smoke or fragrance, hearing knocks on the door, are just a few of the ways the conversation can last forever.

Nothing can take away the pain of losing someone we love, but when we know there are ways to communicate and keep that eternal love from ending, it is such a blessing. I hope this confirmation helps in some small way. I hope you continue to see, feel, and hear these messages of love from the other side. Acknowledge them, and they will get stronger and stronger.

Seeing the Spirit World Proves Life is Eternal

Dear Bonnie: I am trying to figure out what kind of gift I have. Ever since I was 16, I have recalled a woman always whispering my name as if she is trying to get my attention. I was afraid then and would not answer her and run away. I am older now and through the years have had many more experiences.

There was one instance where I was looking into a mirror in our entryway in our home while doing my hair and I saw a woman that looked like she was from the 1800s, based on what she was wearing and her hairstyle. As I looked directly at her, she disappeared.

In another instance, I saw what appeared to be a woman walking toward me. She had an eternal white light glowing from the white clothing that she was wearing. I watched her as she walked into my mother's room. At first, I thought it was my mom, but I found my mom was asleep on the couch when I ran into the living room to find out. I quickly realized I had seen a spirit.

At my family restaurant where I work, I have seen shadows running by, even a woman singing a song. I also can see images of past lives as I blink, and the images flit across my eyes. Clear as day, I can see a vision of a video or picture. I do not want to sound crazy but would like your opinion of what could be happening. I need to find out what this is and what to do with the visions I am seeing. Thanks. — Kate

Dear Kate: Wow! Your story sounds just like my childhood. Seeing clearly into the spirit world and being able to see spirits and even past lives are known as clairvoyance or clear seeing. You described exactly how some with clairvoyance see into the spirit world. Some mediums see videos playing like little movies that they watch inside their minds and then relay what the person in the spirit world was trying to get across to their client by watching those videos. Some see objects, sometimes one object right after another, and can put a story together using those images.

The story of the visitor glowing in white, which you thought was your mom, sounds almost like an experience I had happen to me. I was lying in bed one night while I was young and still living at home when I saw a woman standing in the doorway of my bedroom. I started to yell, "Mom, mom, mom," but the lady who I thought was my mom didn't answer. However, soon my mom came in and asked me why I was yelling.

Thinking back, the figure looked so much like my mom because I realized it was my grandmother in spirit watching over me. Your lady might be your grandmother or even a guide or angel. When the spirit world knows you can see them, the experience starts to happen more often.

It truly is a gift to see the spirit world as it provides proof that life is eternal, and we are a part of the bigger picture. That is why we also can sometimes see past lives as well. A great way to get in touch with our past lives and to make visions stronger is to do meditations and ask the spirit world to show you what you need to know.

I love my gift of seeing, and I hope you genuinely use your gift to help yourself through this life as well as others. Enjoy and embrace your gifts of clear seeing and clear hearing (like hearing the women singing) because it truly is a gift. To learn more, find a teacher or mentor who can help you develop your gifts. When you know more about developing the gifts you have, you will also learn how to control when and where they happen.

A Wink from Heaven

Dear Bonnie: I was standing in a grocery store checkout line when I realized I was thinking about a friend who had recently passed away. As I waited patiently in line for my turn, the memories of my friend and I laughing and enjoying each other's company filled my mind. I was even getting a little teary eyed, then I realized I was next in line.

When I pushed my cart forward and started to unload my groceries, I looked up at the cashier. Her eyes looked exactly like my friend's eyes. She smiled at me, and we started up a conversation as she rung up my groceries. I couldn't help but stare. I am not sure if she saw me staring at her, but I couldn't help myself as her mannerisms were so familiar and reminded me of the way my friend spoke and laughed so easily.

She reminded me of my friend so much I almost asked her if she was a relative of my friend. Am I going mad or do these things really happen? As we finished up the transaction and I paid for my groceries I had this feeling that I had just spent time with my friend, and this was her way of saying "hello." I felt so much better as I walked out the door than I did on the way in. I don't know what this is, but I felt totally at peace. — Julie

Dear Julie: This is one of the ways your loved ones can get a message to you all on their own, no need for a medium.

The spirit world is so smart, and our loved ones know when we need to feel them close. I don't know exactly how they do it, but they can send a person your way in whom they know you will recognize their traits and qualities so similar to theirs it makes you think of them.

It's happened to me a few times and I'm always still amazed.

After my dad passed, I was very sad. I stopped into a convenience store on my way to work. As I started to go in a man that looked to be around my dad's age smiled at me and said, "Hello." I held the door open for him and he said, "You're a gentleman and a scholar." That's something my dad would always say to me, and I would laugh.

My dad was 93 when he passed. This man was around the same age. As he brought his coffee and treats up to the front counter, I had him go before me, and he looked into my eyes with these blue eyes that were piercing even at his older age. My dad and myself were the only ones with blue eyes in the family, so, like you, I was mesmerized by his eyes. Then he said to me, "Aww, you're a sweetheart," again, exactly what my dad always said to me.

Then I realized he was wearing a World War II cap on his head. My dad was also in World War II and always was so proud to wear the hat I purchased for him. I said goodbye to the gentleman. As I made my way to my car, I felt the tears rolling down my face. Yes, that was surely a "wink from Heaven" and truly a sign from my dad, Russell.

May we always be open to hearing and seeing these signs as they are such a gift from heaven.

Family and Relationships

Dear Bonnie: I come from a family of five children. We all seemed to get along and even though we didn't see each other all the time we were happy when we did. It all started going downhill when my mom passed away. She was the glue that kept the family together, but I never really noticed until she passed. I felt a big hole in my heart as my mother was my best friend.

My dad recently passed as well, living only three years after my mom. It was after my dad passed that everything seemed to go wrong between me and my siblings. Everyone seemed to take on roles in the family that they never had before. I know someone has to be in control of finances and selling the house, but it has broken up what we had left of a family. Some of my siblings are no longer talking to each other. I can only imagine what my mom and dad feel in Heaven, seeing their children at odds with one another. Any advice? — Patty

Dear Patty: I certainly do know what it feels like to be in this situation and it's a hard one. I had a similar situation with the passing of my parents. At first, I really let the feelings get to me and I was very sad and upset at one of my brothers, so upset that one night I went to bed thinking of this brother and feeling really angry and hurt.

That's the night that God appeared to me and showed me my brother's face. I asked God why He was showing me his face and He replied, "Because I need you to know a part of me is within him."

Now I was pretty mad at my brother, but when God makes a special trip to give me that news, I am going to listen. You see, every one of us comes from God and He loves us all the same. I know what God was saying, "Love one another even though each of us is not perfect or meant to be."

I counsel people who are grieving when I am giving readings, and what we have both been through is not unfamiliar. In fact, after I had that happen to me in my own family it seemed as though I had so many clients coming in and telling me their stories of what happened in their family after the passing of their parents.

Because I have been through this trying situation as well, I am able to have compassion and sympathy for everyone who is going through this situation. What I know now is how to look at each person's perspective and try to reach deep and find the love that binds us together. It's not easy when we lose our parents, who mean so much to us, but to also lose your siblings is sad beyond words.

Give yourself time to heal and try to stay focused on the love and not the resentment, and soon it gets easier to find the love once again. If God made a special appearance to teach me this lesson in life, it's because He knows I will share it with many. As for your parents and mine who are in Heaven, they know everything that is happening, but they also see the big picture. I know they would want us all to figure this out and come back to love. In the end, the stuff doesn't matter, it's the love.

P.S. I didn't say it would be easy.

Loss is Painful

Dear Bonnie: I have lost people in my life who mean a lot to me, and I know it is painful, but my dad passed this year, and I seem to be having a harder time getting through it. I know it takes time, but I wake up feeling sad about him every morning. I seem to be better during the day at work, but then a thought squeaks in, and I am sad all over. Are there some ways of coping that you can suggest? — Irene

Dear Irene: Loss is a given during our lifetime. Some losses we seem to be able to deal with, and they seem to be more manageable, but others seem to take a hold on our lives and every aspect of it, and the grieving process takes hold of us. Recognizing that you have a loss is the first step and then finding ways to deal with that loss at this moment.

Most of us have felt losses throughout our lives, starting when we were children. A beloved pet, a grandparent that we love, or even moving to a new town and leaving behind friends can be significant losses. As we age, we see loss through divorce, jobs that end, friendships that we had as children disappearing because of time, and growing apart. We mourn for the way things used to be.

The one constant in our lives seems to be our parents, and the idea that they are never going to disappear from our lives. My mom's passing three years ago was a massive loss for me, and I seemed to turn all my energy and focus on helping my dad, who was 90 at the time. It seemed to cushion the despair of losing my mom with caring for my dad. This year I lost my dad, and with no one to take up that time and energy, I felt the loss so much more. The thought that I no longer have parents here on Earth seemed daunting, even to me, a medium who can see spirit on the other side.

Acknowledging your loss first to yourself and then sharing your feelings with others is a big step. There always seems to be someone who knows how you are feeling, and having someone you can openly share your grief with is essential. Holding it inside and letting it fester is not good for your soul or your body.

I do know that life goes on for your dad, just in a different way, and that the bond between the two of you can never be broken. My advice to my clients is to bring their loved ones on their life journey. Your loved ones, in spirit, love it when you are smiling and dancing as they dance by your side. They walk in the sand by the ocean with you and join you as you stand to look out the window, watching the cardinal they have sent your way, one of just a few signs that they are with you still.

I am not a grief counselor, but here are a few tips that might make things a little easier for you.

- Take the time you need to be sad. They're your feelings; acknowledge them.
- Talk to others about your feelings.
- Find a ritual that will help you to honor them.
- Visit the grave if it helps. They hear you no matter what, but if it helps to have a peaceful place to talk to them, they feel honored.
- Plant flowers or a tree in their memory.
- Light a white candle, and say a prayer, as prayers are heard. They say prayers for you as well.
- Create an altar or a place in your home where you can place a picture, play their favorite music, place some flowers, and ask their spirits to join you, then acknowledge their presence. Speak to them like they are there, because they are.
- If a tattoo is your way of keeping them close, they know about this also. It is doing something that makes you feel better.

I remember when my mom passed, I took a pair of her slippers home with me and wore them to bed for a full year. When my husband and I went to see Theresa Caputo, the Long Island Medium, at a big event she was giving, I was amazed to hear her last words before she left the stage: "There is a mom here who wants to acknowledge that her daughter has been wearing her slippers to bed at night for the last year." I loved receiving that message, and it was a piece of evidence that only my mom and I could have known about, confirming for me that she knew my ritual.

I also found relief in going to a spiritualist church that I belong to and receiving messages from my parents from other mediums. Whatever faith you believe in, I feel that the bond with God and the universe helps to lessen the pain in the knowledge that our loved ones are safe and sound. Do what makes you feel better, knowing they are with you still, guiding and watching with love, the kind of love that never leaves us and is everlasting.

At an event I was hosting this past weekend, a husband from the spirit world bent down close to his wife in the audience and handed her a card showing me he was drawing hearts on it. As I explained what I was seeing, the wife said, "Every year my husband made me a handmade Valentine's card that he would draw hearts on and give to me." Who would know that? It was so touching to watch the love that was still so strong between this couple.

I know your loved ones would want me to wish you all a very happy Valetine's Day as they send down their love to you.

Kids Have Close Connections to Those Who Have Passed

Dear Bonnie: My grandmother passed before I was born, but I have always felt a connection to her. My mom had her picture hanging on the wall in our home as I grew up, and I would find myself staring at her picture for the longest time. Now I have a daughter who is just three years old, and she says my grandmother's name out loud and points at her picture like she knows her. What do you think of all this? — Susan

Dear Susan: Many young children can see the spirit world, as they have only been here on Earth for such a short time.

During many readings that I have given in the past, grandparents who have passed will tell me they visit their grandchildren here on Earth. Often a grandparent will tell me they are the one who is having a pretend cup of tea with their granddaughters or are trying to help entertain the little ones while getting to know their grandchildren they did not meet on Earth. Their souls very much know the souls of the children.

I have been shown grandparents rocking a child in their arms and telling me they are the guardians for these children. Grandparents in Heaven often tell me they had known their grandchildren and often held these children long before they came down from Heaven.

I think it is a beautiful thing when someone in heaven can be a spirit guide and mentor from the other side. There is vast opportunity to learn from those who know so much more than we ever could.

I would always encourage a child who is talking about and seeing their spiritual guides or angels and those who watch them and speak about what they are hearing and seeing. The spiritual world only wants what is best for us and offers protection in so many ways.

With so much going on in the world, feeling protected and loved by everyone in spirit who watches over us is just an added benefit of making us feel peace. Say your prayers, as prayers are heard. If you want to feel extra protection at night for yourself and your children, make a bedtime routine that makes you and them feel comforted.

I was giving a reading on Saturday. I had a grandmother in Heaven telling me to have her daughter sing the lullabies to the children that she used to sing but had stopped. It turned out her children were having a hard time sleeping through the night.

I always say those in the spirit world know everything. We need to be aware to receive the signs that help us so much in these trying times.

Home is Where the Heart Is

Dear Bonnie: Due to poor health and financial circumstances, my husband and I have lost the home I inherited from my parents, who have both passed away. This house is also my childhood home, I have lived here all my life.

I do feel my parents' spirits around me, and once, my sister asked for a sign from them while she was taking photos of the house. Later, when she looked at the photos she had taken, she noticed one photo seemed to capture the forms of our parents looking out a window. It looks just like another picture that is among our favorite photographs of them.

Are my parents "stuck" in the house? Are they upset we are leaving the house my father worked so hard to buy? — Bonny

Dear Bonny: Great name! And thank you for your question, and for taking my follow-up call. As soon as you and I connected over the telephone, I saw your mother coming in to communicate. In my mind's eye, she has silvery-gray hair and was sitting because of her end-of-life illness. She showed me the tubes that she had in the end and reassured us that she no longer needs them in Heaven.

Your dad came to stand with her right away, and told me he had dark, thick hair when he was young, although in his later years it became more of a comb-over. He told me that he has been in Heaven longer than your mom, which to me means he was the one to pass away first.

I asked your parents the questions you had wondered about. Your dad spoke first, telling me he had worked hard all his life to comfortably provide for his family. But he was adamant: A house is just an empty shell without the love of family. A house alone does not make a home.

Bonny, your question is a common one. People do wonder if their loved ones in Heaven have an opinion as to how the inheritance they've left was distributed or used. The answer is that unless someone is suffering due to a lack of basic necessities, our loved ones in Heaven view things as just things. Material objects and our notion of success are only Earthly concerns. In Heaven, our loved ones just want to be close to God.

Your dad assured me he is definitely not stuck in the house. He's got a great personality: strong, but jovial. He said, "No one trapped me on Earth, and I am not trapped now!"

This brings up another common question: Do those who have passed on stay in their Earthly home or around their Earthly belongings? I know that sometimes souls are connected to places they love, but I don't think it's like that in most cases. Most of the time the dead will be around their loved ones, wherever they may be, not attached to a particular house.

Next, your mom said she would always stand and watch out the front window because it faced the driveway, and she liked to see who was coming or going. She showed me an image of you, Bonny, rocking in a rocking chair in that very same room.

Your parents showed me a photograph of the two of them when they were first married, all dressed up. Your mother said, "Think of me like this."

Then your father spoke again and asked, "How could Bonny feel that she has let us down? We are so very proud of her and the person and parent she has become." Your mother added that you are a great mom and reassured you that it is okay for you to be a little stricter with the kids.

Bonny, have you noticed the coins your parents have been leaving for you? They are your pennies from Heaven! Your mother added that it is she who has been sending the beautiful birds to you as messengers of her love.

Even though your parents are no longer physically with you, as you can see, their love for you is unchanged and eternal. And now, they have an even greater advantage: They can be with you anytime, anywhere, watching over you and your family.

Can Babies Who Have Passed Communicate with the Living?

Dear Bonnie: I was wondering about babies in Heaven. Can they communicate with you? Does it matter if it was a miscarriage or a child that lived for only a few days? — Tammy

Dear Tammy: I, too, have children from miscarriages in Heaven, and I know that feeling of a hole in your heart.

What was the reason he or she went back home, which is Heaven? Being clairvoyant (seeing), I would get a glimpse of my children in Heaven from time to time. I still always missed them. Then, amazingly, I saw and heard more from them in different ways. Another medium could see my son peeking out behind a computer and smiling. I was able to link in and see him also.

My son told the medium he was sorry, that he very much just wanted to stay in Heaven longer, but loved to be around me as he loved my energy. My son in Heaven looked a lot like my son here on Earth: light skin and red hair and such a nice smile. It did make it easier to bear that he was okay, and it was not my fault, but a choice my son had made.

My daughter's soul would also come to visit very often and stand beside my bed and show herself to me. Again, the reddish hair and beautiful eyes of a little girl would stand next to me. My husband, not understanding me, was awakened in the middle of the night to a little girl who matched my description standing next to the bed. When she realized that he could actually see her, she started to clap her hands out of pure joy, knowing that they had made that connection.

My husband even tried to reach out to her, only to have her vision disappear. I believe she was trying to show him what I was seeing so he would believe also.

I was with a client who came in for a reading and she asked, "Can I hear from my baby who only lived for a few days?" I took a deep breath, not really sure if a baby could communicate, and sure enough, as soon as she got the question out of her mouth, and before I could answer, there was the face of a young woman. I described the young lady and asked if these traits ran in her family. They did.

I wanted to be a clear channel for the woman to talk, and I heard, "That's my mommy"! The number she gave me was the years that she had been in Heaven. Her name was Beth, and she then started to describe in detail the items that her mother had kept since her birth. She showed me a card and described the colors of the beautiful flowers that were on this special card her mom had received when she passed and had kept by her bedside all these years. Beth wanted her mother to know she, too, was very much involved in the lives of her family, even mentioning her sister.

I wasn't sure if a baby that had grown up in Heaven could give me so much evidence, but the evidence came through loud and clear, and the tears were flowing. Her mom told me she had waited all this time to be able to communicate with her little girl, who had grown into a beautiful young woman on the other side.

This also was a lesson for me because I was not sure, myself. But you see, a soul is a soul, and there is no time in Heaven, only the unconditional love of family.

Please know that if our children are in Heaven, they very much are around you and living life with you, even though it is not in the physical plane. Knowing that our children are okay in Heaven makes the pain of that hole in your heart a little easier to bear.

Does Suicide Keep You Out of Heaven?

Dear Bonnie: My son passed away two months ago, and I want to have a reading done, but I've been told that he might not be in Heaven or able to communicate with me because he chose to take his life. My hope is that you can shed some light on this with me and tell me if this is true or not. My heart is broken, and I desperately want to know if he is okay. Thank You, Carly.

Dear Carly: As a full-time professional medium who gives readings daily, I unfortunately see these circumstances more frequently than you would think. It is such a sad scenario that needs to be talked about openly. Everyone goes to Heaven, but especially those who need God's white light. There is no stigma in Heaven, and I always tell everyone God would not forsake his children.

When I was just in my twenties, and I had not started doing mediumship sessions, I had a very sweet friend who was like my little sister who committed suicide. Chris was very intelligent and sensitive, and I was very involved in all of her life's big events. I did her makeup for her prom and was there for her graduation from high school.

Chris was just 18 and had been accepted to the college of her choice. She was very excited to be going away to college. She had the whole world ahead of her. She and her dad were very active in target practice with guns, and that's a hobby they would do together often. The guns were kept in the house under lock and key, so they were very responsible, but Chris knew where the key was.

Chris had the same boyfriend for two years, and that first love was very intense. Everything was fine until Chris's boyfriend wanted to break things off with her, and he even brought a date into the restaurant we both worked at. I saw her fall apart, but there was nothing I could do, and we were both so young. I didn't know, however, how much pain she was in or the fact she just couldn't take that pain. Chris's mom found her on her bed, where she had shot herself in the head with her dad's gun.

I was heartbroken for everyone, and I had the same feelings as many do; what if I had done this or said that or tried harder? I still, to this day, wish I could have done more. I cried so hard, and my heart ached so badly. A few nights later I went to bed, and I asked Chris a question before falling asleep. Soon, my third eye opened, which is the way we see into the spirit world, and there was my beautiful Chris telling me she was okay and not to worry. She made sure to show me her beautiful face where she was perfect and not harmed in any way.

Chris was relieving my worries about her not being okay, but there she was, just as beautiful and loving as always. That was my first experience with suicide. I believe God now sends me parents and loved ones who have lost someone to suicide because of my deep belief and my own experience with suicide.

I have seen my friend in my dreams and other mediums have brought Chris through during readings where she will appear and tell them to tell me she loves me too, but she is busy in Heaven helping others who have chosen to end their life as well. Chris will use her experience now to help others.

There is no judgment in Heaven; God will never forsake his children because of our choices. There is definitely significant healing of our minds and souls in Heaven. Clients who come for a session can be assured that those who have made the choice to leave this world early are not penalized.

Hearing from those in Heaven who have committed suicide, I do hear them say they are sorry for hurting those whom they left behind and the grief they have caused. Many tell me they were not thinking as they should have been, and they feel bad for those whom they left behind.

As a medium, I can tell you they come through with the same personalities and with all the love they have for their families, the same as everyone else who is on the higher side of life. They come through with a new understanding, no addictions, no ailments, just their beautiful soul unharmed.

Families Can Be Tough

Dear Bonnie: The holidays are coming. How do I keep the peace with my family members while staying true to myself and my beliefs? My family can be very opinionated, and I am already feeling my nerves and anxiety kicking in. I don't want to stay away because I do love my family, but I always seem to end up with hurt feelings. It seems even harder now that my mother has passed. Any suggestions would be helpful. — Cara

Dear Cara: The holidays can be a tough time for almost every family. I believe we all have the right to our own beliefs, and it would be nice for family members that are getting together for a celebration to honor those around them. Families can be the hardest to get along with because we are here to learn valuable lessons from each other.

Keeping the peace with our family members during holiday gatherings can be full of anxiety and stress, and to many, the sadness of lost loved ones who will not be joining us around the table or at the gathering can be as painful as the day we lost them. Try to imagine how they are feeling and find only compassion for them. Our lives are made up of memories, and when we are missing someone, special emotions can stir, and it's not really about who is gathered but who is in the room.

We can feel angry that we no longer have that special person with us. We don't know what is going on inside someone's heart or mind that could be making them behave badly. We need to pull out all our compassion and wisdom to know when to speak and when to hold our tongue. Try to be as understanding as you can but without giving away your contentment. We need to take care of ourselves first. Keep those who are pulling you into their drama at a distance and send them light and love.

Just remember the Golden Rule: Treat others as we would like to be treated. Look to your heart to find kindness and compassion for those who do not understand or are missing the tools in their toolbox to recognize pure love without putting restrictions on others. Stay away from the naysayers trying to bring others down so that they may feel better about themselves. Forgive them, Lord, for they know not what they do.

The celebrations that are coming up have beautiful meanings to them.

Try to get your guest or hostess focused on the meaning of the holidays instead of themselves and their current situation. Unconditional love is about honoring yourself and others. Be that person that God made you to be and remember that this too shall pass. Keep these words from the Bible in your heart, Cara: Love is patient, love is kind.

Here are some tips for guarding and protecting your energy while going to any gathering or party during the holidays:

1. First, picture a beautiful white light coming up through the soles of your feet, God's beautiful, healing, white light. The light comes up through the soles of your feet and then, like a ribbon, starts to wrap around your ankles, calves, legs, stomach, chest and back, shoulders and neck, and right up to the top of your head (your crown chakra). This beautiful white light of protection is like a hug from God and a shield from Archangel Michael. Picture this white light while at the same time asking for protection from any hurtful thoughts or feelings coming your way. Ask for only joy and happiness to surround you.
2. Ground your energy before leaving the house so you feel connected to Mother Earth, becoming centered and relaxed. Picture a beautiful ball of green light starting at the top of your head and coming down into the crown chakra, your forehead, throat, heart, stomach, legs, and arms, and feeling this ball of light releasing any nerves or anxiety that you are feeling down to Mother Earth. The green ball of light continues down through the soles of your feet going down 12 inches into Mother Earth. You are now grounded.
3. Remember James Billet Freeman's prayer of protection:
   The light of God surrounds me;
   The love of God enfolds me;
   The power of God protects me;
   The presence of God watches over me;
   For wherever I am, God is!

Cara, I hope these tips help make your gatherings filled with light and love. Happy holidays! Blessings, Bonnie.

Do Mom and Dad Take Sides?

Dear Bonnie: With the start of the holiday season coming soon and family gatherings close by, I was wondering if you could share your thoughts on family conflict. Do you believe parents who are in Heaven take sides over their adult children who are not getting along? My sister and I have not been able to get along after a recent conflict, and I am wondering what my parents would say. Would they stick up for me? — Ann

Dear Ann: I have had several clients come in and ask me this same question. It's not that uncommon for someone to come for a reading and want to connect with a parent with these same thoughts in mind. They want to know if their mom or dad agrees with them on a certain matter and want to be consoled on what they are going through with one or more siblings.

We all know that these difficult relationships with our siblings can serve to teach us some very hard lessons, and it's not so easy to go through the process of finding peace. Please know that no family is perfect, and if we try to achieve perfection or our idea of what a family is supposed to look or act like, we might be greatly disappointed. Every family can have drama, but it is up to us how we respond to it. We have no control over how others react, only our response.

Getting back to your question, whenever I have been giving a reading and had a client ask, "What does my mother think of how my sister or brother has been treating me?" I pause because I know what they want to hear. We all want to hear that our siblings have made bad choices or decisions, that we are in the right and want our parents' support and for them to stick up for us on the other side.

I always ask and listen to what a mom or dad has to say, but it rarely sounds close to what we expect. You see, Heaven is all about unconditional love, and there is no judgment. That doesn't mean a parent wants to see a child in harm's way, but when it comes to pointing fingers, they just don't do it. They have a better view of a situation than we do, and they look into the soul of their child here on Earth to see why this sort of behavior is happening.

We don't always know why our siblings are striking out at us or trying to hurt our feelings, but by looking at that person as a soul instead of just a sibling, we sometimes are better able to see where they are coming from.

Every parent here or in Heaven wants their children to get along and love each other. It's the best gift you can give your parents. Nothing makes them happier than seeing their children showing love for each other. There are lots of reasons why grown children can be at odds with each other. Feelings of jealousy or rivalry are just a couple of them.

But what seems most important to parents is that their children can find a way to be at peace with one another. When parents are gone, it's the children who are left with the task of keeping the family held closely together. If the parent was the glue that held the family together, the family can start to unravel.

What can you do to keep your family close? Try to find peace, even if it means you are the peacemaker. Try not to pass judgment on your siblings or their children. Remember, everyone is on their own journey here and might not always meet the expectations you have for them. Try to make your siblings see they are important to you, sharing your struggles and accomplishments with them.

Try to stay connected, even if it's just a phone call. If there's a problem, try to get to the root of it as soon as possible by being honest and asking, "Why are you behaving this way towards me?" Work with them to find a solution. Where there's a problem, there usually is a solution if you look deep inside your heart. If you have created wounds, try to heal them. Healing can take time. All you can do is your best.

Remember that your siblings have been with you throughout your lifetime. It would be sad to let differences get in the way.

There Are No Grudges in Heaven

Dear Bonnie: Can a person who passed have a negative effect on someone here if they passed holding on to a grudge or worse? Can they have a negative effect on the living? — Brenda

Dear Brenda: That's a very good question! I bet a lot of people think about this question but never seem to ask about it. I myself had wondered about this very same question before I became more familiar with how Heaven works.

Say you had a relationship that didn't end too well or maybe a divorced spouse that you had not come to any reconciliation with, and they were still holding onto jealously, anger or even had hate in their heart. How would that affect you here? We hope that this is not the scenario, but this is Earth, and we are here to learn lessons so our soul can become complete.

What if someone didn't learn the lesson of forgiveness before they passed? I can tell you with confidence that I have never heard a spirit say, "I'm still angry." When we pass, we go through this beautiful transition to a higher plane and we have a life review. That's where we see and feel everything that we have done to ourselves and others on our journey here.

Every time we said hurtful things or did something out of meanness, our review shows us how we made the other person feel, not so that we are judged, but rather only to see how we could have handled the situation differently. We now get to see the bigger picture and why some things happened the way they did. They were all lessons.

When we enter the Heavenly realm, all those bad, heavy emotions are taken away. No more are we holding on to, "Why did this or that happen to me?" or "Why was I treated this way?" Those emotions are no longer held onto, almost like a big weight being lifted off our shoulders. We feel relief.

Spirits tell me they do have regrets for their wrongdoings and very much want to tell that person or family member, "Hey, I'm so sorry for my actions or my part in the relationship that went bad. I now know I'm sorry and I wish for forgiveness." Unconditional love is all you're going to receive from Heaven because that is what Heaven is all about, the unconditional love for yourself and others.

Brenda, do not have the fear that someone who has passed can do any harm to you here on Earth, because that just won't happen. If you have had someone who has passed and you weren't on good terms with them while they were here, be the bigger person and send them love and light up to Heaven. It not only releases heavy emotions that you are carrying in your heart, but also helps their soul to feel the forgiveness and continue to grow.

You don't need to condone something bad that someone has done to you or someone holding a grudge against you, but you do need to release the emotion and let it go for your own sake and well-being. Send a prayer up to Heaven that you forgive them and move on, feeling confident that only love comes from Heaven.

Alzheimer's Patients Forgive Their Children Once They Have Passed

Dear Bonnie: I was wondering about people who have Alzheimer's. We had to put my mom in a nursing home, and she had this disease. I often feel regret and worry that she did not understand, as she passed in her sleep at this nursing home. It leaves my heart heavy. Do you think she knew this was our only option? — Pauline

Dear Pauline: I know your mom would not want you to feel regret at the choices you needed to make. I often have clients that come in wondering if their parents who had Alzheimer's could understand or hear the words that were spoken to them. I can assure you that even though it didn't seem that they could hear in the physical world, their soul heard every word that was spoken or whispered in their ear.

Your mom knows the love and concern you had for her and the love you hold in your heart. Our bodies may not last forever, but our soul is eternal and carries all the information within us. Our soul has had many lifetime journeys and will continue until the day we decide we have learned all the lessons we want to learn, as our soul continues to expand and learn from each lifetime here on Earth.

We come down to Earth with our soul family, which was formed before our journey began. You picked your mom and dad and the rest of your family, (yes, even your siblings), for the lessons and things your soul wanted to learn in this lifetime. Your siblings and soul family can be here to teach you some of those toughest lessons. The Earth is our school room, a place to learn, and Heaven is our home. It's hard to think we picked certain lessons to learn while here this time on Earth.

Making tough decisions might have been something you chose to learn so your soul would recognize certain aspects of feelings and emotions. As we learn the lessons that we chose here, our hearts and souls open up to greater knowledge and love. We understand what it feels like to have had to make hard decisions that affect others.

If we look at the circumstances that happen to us in our everyday lives, we start to realize there is a lesson in almost every choice or situation that is happening to us. As we look deep into our trials and tribulations, we can try to decipher what lessons are hidden in the problems we are experiencing.

Many people go through life trying to learn the same lessons, making the same mistakes in their lives over and over again until one day a lightbulb goes off and they see the lesson for what it is. This is when they can see the lesson and learn from it. Every lesson is not a punishment, but a way for our soul to keep growing.

I often tell my clients that if there were no trials and tribulations in our lives, and everything was always happy and carefree, our souls would not be able to learn the valuable lessons that we all came down here to learn.

Our hearts and souls open up and expand as we learn empathy and how to feel compassion and sympathy for others. It makes us better people when we know how others are feeling, and we feel for them. We all are learning these lessons. When we realize what the lesson is, we can say, "Thank you. I understand," handle it with grace, and then ask that the lesson be taken away.

When we get to heaven is when we find out in our life review how we did with the lessons we chose, not to judge, but to see where we handled things and learned from them, or how we could have done better.

I tell clients, "Learn your lesson this time around so your soul can grow, and you don't have to bring the same lesson with you the next time you come back to the Earth plane."

I am not immune to these lessons myself. I know how hard it is to have a parent who has Alzheimer's and has to be in a care facility. I now understand the lesson of having no control over certain situations and having to surrender to that feeling. I know why I had to learn that lesson, as I always want to be in control. There is a deep-hearted feeling when you seem to have no control over what is happening in your life and the feelings that come with it. I now understand this.

Know in your heart that you did the very best with your mom in the situation you were given. Our parents only feel the love we have for them, and their souls know the lessons that had to be learned. Heaven is our home, and their souls are now free from any disability and illnesses they had while here on Earth.

I used to tell my father, who was brought up having horses, "Dad, you get to have all your horses back when you get to Heaven," and he would say, "I'll have a herd." I see him now in Heaven, and when he shows up, he brings his horses with him.

They are now watching out for us and hear our thoughts and prayers, so have no regrets. It's only the love that matters.

My Childhood Home

Dear Bonnie: I am having a hard time saying goodbye to my family home and moving on. Do you think this is crazy? I have all these emotions. — Ginger

Dear Ginger: I absolutely know what you are going through. I am so sorry. I know it's hard, as I am going through the same thing, and I am sure others have had these same feelings.

This week was a hard week for me as I had to say goodbye to the family home that I was brought up in. My mother and father purchased a one-room schoolhouse almost 70 years ago. The home is listed in the history books as dating back to 1886. My mom, always being proud of this fact, kept the sign showing this by the front door.

My mom passed three years ago, and my dad left everything in the house perfectly the same. When he went to Heaven a few months ago, my sister and brothers and I needed to go in and clear everything out of the house so we could put it on the market. So much of me wanted to keep that house for myself, but it just wasn't in the cards.

Walking in, I knew it would be daunting without seeing my mom or dad waiting for me to come in, as there was always a hug and kiss waiting inside for me. I moved out of the house at a pretty young age, my mom handing me a key and saying, "A woman should always have a place to go, and this will always be your home."

On the last visit, because the house had sold, I felt the pull to go in and say a few words and thank my mom and dad for being such great parents and raising us in an environment where I always felt safe and loved, in a house that was filled with so many memories.

I was one child of five children, and I can still remember us having different bedrooms as the older siblings grew and moved out of the house. I walked through the hall and felt the woodwork for the last time, and not just any woodwork. These boards were the old-fashioned kind. I could feel the energy of all the years I had laughed, cried, and told stories here, not to mention all the spirits that had kept me company.

I went through each room recalling a particular memory of me being in there with each person in my family. I went into the first bedroom that I could remember sleeping in and looked into the closet. In there I found the pink, flowered wallpaper I loved so much, as I remembered laying in my bed as a young girl, daydreaming, looking at the beautiful flowers.

I walked outside and said goodbye to my grandmother's rose bush that still bloomed each year as well as the flower bed my mom loved so much. As I was looking around, my eyes gazed at my dad's apple tree, and I found myself thinking, who will take care of his beloved tree and his blueberry bushes? My dogs and cats all buried under the trees around the same spot. I know they are not there, but who will ever know that they lived and were loved?

Leaving the house for the last time and taking just the memories, I wished and hoped the new owner will feel the love that comes from this house and all the love that went on inside.

I read that walking around the house or home you are leaving and telling the house that you are going and someone new is coming releases the energy you have given it and helps the house to welcome the new people that hopefully will love it as you have.

Complicated Relationships

Dear Bonnie: I had a complicated relationship with a relative who was not a perfect person in life. When she died, we had been estranged for many years. If Heaven isn't a place where grudges exist, what happens when she passes with unresolved relationship issues? Is it safe to assume that the other person is all set and forgives (and is forgiven for) the toxic relationship? — Gia

Dear Gia: This question comes up all the time! First, no one on Earth is perfect. It is our schoolroom, and we are here to learn and grow from mistakes. If we were perfect, we wouldn't be on Earth in the first place!

Because no one is perfect, naturally, when we die, many of us leave with unfinished business. When we go to Heaven, we are given a life review where we are shown the major choices we made during life. We see it all: the good we have done, where we have lifted others up and made the world a better place, and also the decisions that were hurtful and failed others.

During this review, we actually feel what it felt like for someone when we hurt them. We are given this life review not to be judged, but so that we can learn from our lives. Remember, Earth is our schoolroom and life is our education.

When recalling a situation with someone with whom you've had a difficult relationship, ask yourself and ask God, "What lesson do I need to learn from this?" By reframing your perspective in this way, the life lesson will become clear. Sometimes you'll learn patience or to be humble, sometimes you'll learn acceptance, and sometimes you'll learn the value of self-care and setting boundaries. Once that lesson is realized, you'll find the situation stops happening. The life lesson has been learned, and you can move on.

I was taught by a famous medium that we must do our best to leave for Heaven without any regrets. If we extend our hand for forgiveness and it is not accepted, then it is no longer our baggage. It is that of the person who did not accept our apology. Always try to be the bigger person. Always try to make or accept an apology.

Yes, you can make amends in the afterlife! It is incredibly healing for all involved. I have seen so many people leave a reading with me with a new light in their hearts, unburdened at last because they were able to say or hear "I'm sorry." I have also seen those in heaven finally be able to communicate what is in their heart to their loved ones here on Earth. They heal, too, and once they convey their message, their soul is able to move on from the situation and continue to grow.

Heaven is all about unconditional love, but people are people on Earth as in Heaven. So, try to make amends for mistakes or hurt feelings, because you do not want to be here or in Heaven with regrets.

Only You Can Decide Who Should Be in Your Life

Dear Bonnie: I want to make some changes in my life, and I am not sure how to go about this without ending relationships that seem to drag me down instead of lifting me up. How do I know for sure who should I keep in my life and who should I let go of? — Judy

Dear Judy: One of my tasks as a spiritual life coach is to help others see who is draining their energy. To make the changes you want, you first need to decide who is bringing your energy down.

Sit down with a pen and paper and make a list of everyone in your life: family, friends, co-workers, etc., and then beside each of their names check off who nurtures your soul and who doesn't. The best way to do this is to feel it within you. Sit with your eyes closed and begin to say each of their names in your mind.

What feelings arise in your heart when you picture their face or say their name? This exercise is the first indicator of who is supporting you on your journey and who is not invested in your future. By doing this exercise you will begin to sense and feel who is draining your power.

Energy drainers are people who lack their vitality, so they need or want yours. People sometimes want what you have but don't want to put in the work to get to where you are in life or your job. These are the people who often have their agenda and are leaning on you to get to where they want to be.

Be aware of those around you who are just trying to get something from you. If someone is gossiping with you, they are most likely gossiping about you, too. They may appear to be sweet and kind while taking your energy and using it as their own.

You want people in your life who lift you up, not drain you. There are always going to be people who are jealous of what others have, but they don't want to put in the work to have what you do. They might want to be fit but don't want to go to the gym, or they may want to have a clean, uncluttered home, but don't want to take the time or energy to do this for themselves.

Here are some examples of how you might feel if someone is draining your energy. You might experience sleeplessness, a feeling of fear, negative emotions, uneven emotions, low self-esteem, low confidence, moodiness, or over-sensitivity. It might even affect your diet by craving carbs and sugar as a way of bringing your energy up.

We want to identify the people who have this effect on us and make some changes. Just seeing someone in your life with a new understanding will set you free to decide who stays in your life or who you choose to spend less time with.

Remember, it's all about our journey and making the best and most well-informed decisions. Sometimes it is about bringing these emotions to the surface and then going from there.

Living our best life starts with who we let in our lives. Everyone who comes into your life is a lesson to be learned or a teacher. It's up to you to decipher who is who.

Leaving a Relationship

Dear Bonnie: How can I cut cords with my ex-girlfriend so we both can move on from this relationship? We both want to move on, but it feels like we are stuck. We have broken up several times and we always get back together; however, we are miserable once again after a few weeks. Can you give me the directions for cord cutting? — Chuck

Dear Chuck: So many people just like you need to cut cords of attachments. They might not be from a girlfriend or boyfriend, but these cords could be from other people's energy, such as the energy of those who seem to drain you when you are having a conversation.

Some people who are empaths seem to have energy from others attach their energy rather easily. Print this column and keep these directions, and make sure to give yourself some time to clear others' energy away from you. You can make it as elaborate or simple as you choose. Maybe you set up a special place, light a candle, burn some sage, whatever makes you comfortable.

What are these cords?

We all can form "energetic" cords that attach themselves to us and stay in our aura (energy field) and drain the energy from us, causing emotional stress or even addictions. Cords can be made from emotions and their energy.

Where do the cords come from?

We can have cords attached to a person, an object, or any situation. Two people who are in a relationship, family members, work relationships, a past life, a friendship, or even a spouse or a loved one who has passed away can share these cords of attachment.

Why do we get them?

We all have them. They are normal but, ideally, we just want and need our energy without someone else getting in our way or dragging us down. Our chakra centers send out and receive energy every day, so we have the tendency to attract these cords.

Some cords are out of love, and some come because of a trauma, such as a breakup. Some come from ill feelings of anger and unforgiveness. When these cords are attached to us, we might feel the other person's emotions and therefore not feel quite ourselves and become out of balance.

We could feel a sense of stress and a strain on our being. We can also pick up these cords from our environment, such as the workplace. The best we can do for ourselves is to pay attention to our bodies and minds and become attuned to when our emotions do not seem like our own.

A Reiki healer will know how to see or feel a cord and know how to remove it, but here are some tips you can try at home. If you feel like you need more help, make an appointment with a reiki master.

Cord cutting

Cord cutting is a simple tool to remove, dissolve, and heal the emotional, energetic energy that has become attached to you. This procedure has no actual physical cutting as it is all energetically done. They are cut and healed with energy.

Create A Space: Find a place that is quiet and peaceful. Make it your own sanctuary. Play soft music, burn a candle, use some essential oils, or put flowers in a vase. Make it a comfortable and safe place for you.

Start the Healing: Take a few deep breaths, inhale through your nose, and imagine a white light of healing entering your body. Then exhaling through your mouth, picture a fine gray mist containing everything you no longer need to hold on to exiting your body. This is actually the cutting away of unhealthy emotional energy that can keep oneself unable to break loose from a situation or to be able to think clearly.

Call in Archangel Michael: He will assist you with his sword of light and love that will gently cut away the cords that have attached to you while at the same time sending them back with love and healing to the places and situations to which they were originally attached. You are safe. You are protected.

- Closing your eyes, scan your energetic field to see if you can see or feel any dense, hot, or cold areas in your auric field. Feel any emotions that come to the surface.
- Try to locate where the cords are attached. They might be found in your heart center, solar plexus, sacral chakra, or in several places. Some might be larger than others. They can also range in color from light to dark, with the dark being more of a problem energetically.
- Feel the divine energy filling every cell and organ in your body. This is a healing experience as Archangel Michael begins to cut the cords away. You might begin to feel sensations or even emotions of relief or an emotional bond being lifted. Archangel Michael will heal the energetic holes that have been created, filling them with white light.

Thank Archangel Michael: Thank Archangel Michael for the healing and end with a prayer of thanks. Be sure to drink plenty of water, rest and relax.

- Enjoy the feeling that this exercise can bring to you. Do this exercise once or twice a month or whenever you feel the need.

Relationships that Just Won't Work

Dear Bonnie: I have a relationship in my family that does not work out no matter how hard I try. I know you talk about soul families and how we choose our parents. So, what could this mean for me? I have tried everything I can think of to make peace, but as hard as I try, it just does not happen. Any advice? — Matthew

Dear Matthew: It is true that we all pick our parents and our soul family. Before we come to Earth, we ask some of our soul family to reincarnate with us so we might learn valuable lessons that help each of us grow and expand with the knowledge of love and compassion.

We do not know what lessons we choose, because that memory is taken away when we are born. So, if we look at each relationship in the way of what lesson we might be learning, it can sometimes shine a light on what we might learn from each, even though it might be difficult to understand.

So here is the tricky part: when we come down for another turn at life and growth, we also have free will. Free will plays a big part in our journey, because that free will is yours and will never be taken away. Choices we make of our own free will cannot change unless we see another way into a situation or challenge.

We cannot want something for someone else that they do not want for themselves. It just does not happen. What lesson might that be? A lesson of compassion for the person that we love that is not making the best decisions for themselves because they cannot see what we might see. It is everybody's journey of learning for themselves.

Think of how many parents want more for their children, but their children might have chosen an unhealthy lifestyle. Unless the child is willing to take the steps and put in the effort to be healthier, a parent can be left helpless, wondering what went wrong and why. So many sessions I give are to parents who have a child with an addiction. They wonder why it happened and what they could have done differently, and they carry that burden.

The lesson here might be one of the hardest. They are doing everything they can for that child, but that child has free will. The lesson might be I cannot change another person, so I love them unconditionally as they are. Heaven is where we review our life and how each decision changed our lives, and the ones who were affected by those choices.

Mediumship sessions, where a son might be coming through telling me to "please tell my mom I am sorry, but tell her I am no longer addicted," can be very healing for my client and for the son coming through from the higher side of life to be able to have a voice and get a message across.

If you have relationships in your family that are not working out, give them a good look and see what lesson you might have asked to learn but remember, free will is their choice, and we cannot take that away but just encourage others on this road called life. We can only do what we can do, and we only have power over ourselves. Some things might not be worked out in this lifetime and will have to wait until the next. It is all a journey.

Family and Friends Who Don't Believe

Dear Bonnie: I am very spiritual, and I offer tarot cards at psychic fairs. I am very proud of my work, but when I am around certain people or family members, I hide what I do, as they tend to criticize and attack me with their beliefs. I see that you are very public about what you do. Can you give me some advice for handling family, friends and those who do not believe? — Shirley

Dear Shirley: We cannot change the way the public or friends and families feel about what we do. I was asked by God to share my gift and to shine light into a world that is filled with more darkness every day. I know it's hard when we get criticized or attacked by someone that just doesn't understand. This also happens to people who don't do what we do. This easily can go right to our heart space, and once that happens it's easy to fall into the rabbit hole of feeling not good enough, feeling victimized and not loved.

My dad used the old saying, "Stop stewing over it." That's what can happen when we get into that space of not feeling validated or seen for who we are. We let into our minds space all the negativity that is around us and we take it in internally, and it rolls around and around in our thoughts until we are able to view it in another light and kick these unloved feelings out of our space.

Now I didn't say it was easy to do, but here are a few ways of giving those negative feelings that we are holding onto the boot.

It starts with taking a step back and taking a mental break from it all. Meditation, deep breathing, walking outside, playing uplifting music, maybe some yoga, saying a prayer or affirmations, anything that is uplifting.

I like to go shopping. It seems to tame my thoughts and gets me out of the space my mind wants to linger in. It's not just the shopping, though. It's taking the time to smile at other people, maybe chat with someone who I have never met. It's all about changing the thoughts that keep stewing in our mind. It is giving ourselves a mental break from our worries and getting back to truly feeling one with God and the universe.

Giving ourselves respite from the daily concerns in life is like going on a vacation. You're going to come home after a week, but when you do you start with a new perspective. As we give ourselves this break, everyday things seem less critical and easier to handle. As for those people in the world that do not honor you for you, well, that's a choice we all need to make at some point as far as who we really want to surround ourselves with.

As for the critics, some people are scared and not educated in today's metaphysical world and they let that fear get in the way of truly understanding our work, but don't let that persuade you to give up something that you love. When our work is done with love and integrity there should be no shame. Being a bright light in a world that is becoming darker by offering guidance to those who need help is an honor, and that is how I truly look at what I do.

The Story of Lucky

Dear Bonnie: I have been seeing spirit out of the corner of my eyes and wondering if this is possible. I usually dream about my loved ones, but seeing while I am awake is starting to get stronger. Can you tell me more about these visions? — **Jake**

Dear Jake: We all have the ability to connect to the other side. There are two ways of seeing spirit: objectively and subjectively. Objectively is to see while your eyes are open and subjectively is while you are dreaming or seeing inside your mind through your third eye, located in the middle of your forehead. It is rarer to see spirit with your eyes open, but it does happen.

Let me tell you about one of my first times seeing outside of my third eye. When I was 12, I had a dog named Lucky. He was a small mixed breed. I had been asking for a dog for a long time until my father gave in and we came home with him. Lucky and I grew together and, being my first dog, we were very connected. He was a very active and free-spirited dog. He would sleep by my bed at night, and I always had my hand hanging off the side to be touching him. He also had a box of toys next to him to console his need to chew. He was a very happy dog.

I would always say goodbye as I got on the bus that came to take me to school each day, but this one particular day, I felt rushed as I was late getting started for my day and didn't take the time for our morning goodbyes, thinking I would see him soon. One of my greatest joys was Lucky waiting for me to get home from school, but this day would stay with me through life.

Arriving home from school, I rushed in the house to find Lucky was nowhere to be found and started to call for him when my dad delivered the sad news that Lucky had gotten out the front door and had run out into the road and been struck by a car and had passed away. I was devastated. I cried and felt especially sad having not said goodbye to him that morning. I felt the pain and guilt that maybe he ran out looking for me.

My parents rarely left me alone, but one afternoon, a week after Lucky's passing, they let me stay home as they went to do an errand. Coming out of my bedroom and heading into the living room, next to the fireplace I saw Lucky. I couldn't believe what I was seeing. He was sitting there bright as day with a big smile on his lips and wagging his tail. He was so happy I could see him.

I shouted his name and headed over to pat him, and I almost reached him when he disappeared. I couldn't believe what had just happened. I was so excited to see Lucky with that smile on his face and to see him so happy and very much alive. Our connection, I am sure, made this happen. He needed me to know he was okay even though we no longer could be together in the psychical world.

Heading back into my room, I looked down to see Lucky's toys out of the closet. My mom had put them away so as not to be a reminder, and to my surprise, they were newly chewed with tiny new bites in them, and they were placed all around the room. I couldn't even believe what I was seeing.

I left the toys as they were to show my mom that Lucky had come to visit. My mom, being a medium herself, was amazed that Lucky had such energy that he left proof of his visit. Being a little girl, it didn't take all the pain away, but it surely helped knowing he was safe in Heaven and very much alive.

I don't see outside, or objectively, as much as I used to, but it sure is a gift. Now it's more controlled as to looking inside my third eye to see. If you are seeing outside your peripheral vision and seeing signs from spirit, welcome them, and your spirit sightings will get stronger.

Another way of seeing that is very common is in dreams. If they seem real and you can see colors or you find yourself having a conversation with a loved one in Heaven, it's a visit, and one you don't want to miss. Keep a journal and a pen next to your bed and write down your visions as soon as you can to remember these precious moments.

Losing a Pet is hard, but Remember the Joy it Brought

Dear Bonnie: How can I help my daughter get over the death of her guinea pig? — Sandy

When a pet dies, a child can feel absolutely devastated! The loss of a pet can feel like the death of a family member. Unfortunately, the joy of owning a pet goes hand in hand with the heartbreak of losing one.

Sandy explained to me that her daughter was uncertain if her guinea pig would go to Heaven and needed to know Twinkle would be okay. I had not talked to a guinea pig before, but a soul is a soul. So, I tuned into spirit and almost immediately Twinkle showed up, munching on something a guinea pig would eat! I was amazed with the clarity that Twinkle could communicate with me. I often speak with cats and dogs, but this was new to me.

So, you ask, what could a guinea pig have to say? Quite a lot of information came pouring out of this little animal's mouth. He told me he had loved the times that Stephanie would rush home only to run to his cage and sit with him while she told him stories of how her day had gone at school, how he never felt lonely because he had not one but two other friends in the same cage with him.

Twinkle continued to give me a list of all the foods he used to enjoy and how he had had a happy life full of joy. To Stephanie, her furry animal was more like a family member that she had trusted and cared for. Their long talks had helped her in times when she needed someone to listen. Twinkle wanted me to let Stephanie know he would see her again someday but until that time to enjoy his other friends that were still in her care. He felt loved and was very grateful for their time together.

Tips to help a child deal with death:

- When the death of a pet occurs in the family, it usually affects each member in his or her own way.
- With children, when talking about death, use simple, clear words that they can understand, depending on the age of the child.

- Don't assume that every child understands death in the same way or with the same emotions or feeling.
- To a child, a pet may be their first friend. All children are different, and their view of the world is unique and shaped by their own experiences. Grieving is a process.
- Listen to them, offering comfort and support.
- Help them to remember stories about their beloved pet.
- If it helps, ask the child if they would like to have a funeral for the pet and let them be a part of the service while saying goodbye.
- There is a poem called "Rainbow Bridge" (author unknown) that is pretty well- known and may help to ease the pain your child is feeling.

"Rainbow Bridge"

Just this side of heaven is a place called Rainbow Bridge. When an animal dies that has been especially close to someone here, that pet goes to Rainbow Bridge. There are meadows and hills for all of our special friends so they can run and play together. There is plenty of food, water and sunshine, and our friends are warm and comfortable.

All the animals who had been ill and old are restored to health and vigor. Those who were hurt or maimed are made whole and strong again, just as we remember them in our dreams of days and times gone by. The animals are happy and content, except for one small thing; they each miss someone very special to them, who had to be left behind.

They all run and play together, but the day comes when one suddenly stops and looks into the distance. His bright eyes are intent. His eager body quivers. Suddenly he begins to run from the group, flying over the green grass, his legs carrying him faster and faster.

You have been spotted, and when you and your special friend finally meet, you cling together in joyous reunion, never to be parted again. The happy kisses rain upon your face; your hands again caress the beloved head, and you look once more into the trusting eyes of your pet, so long gone from your life but never absent from your heart. Then you cross Rainbow Bridge together.

Author Unknown

Sandy, I hope this helps you to make Twinkle's passing a little easier for your daughter. Please tell Stephanie to watch for Twinkle in her dreams, as they often come to visit when in a dream state, letting their friend know that they are safe and happy.

Animals in Heaven

Dear Bonnie: I am heartbroken over my dog Sandy's passing. She grew old and frail, and I made the wrenching decision to end her pain and have her put down. My son had a close connection with her, too. We had Sandy cremated and keep the ashes at home. Recently, I disturbed my beloved dog's ashes so my son could put some of those ashes into a special locket. Was that wrong of me? — Carol.

Dear Carol: Thank you for granting me permission to speak to Sandy in Heaven and thank you for this photograph of her! What a beautiful golden retriever. In Heaven Sandy is vibrant and full of youthful energy again. She bounded right up to me!

Carol, Sandy told me that she calls you Momma, and showed me that in her Earthly life she had quite a bit of energy then, too. Sandy wants to reassure you that you made the right decision to end her suffering. She showed me her hind legs as the source of her pain and the reason for her passing.

Please don't feel guilty for "disturbing" her ashes. Although the sentiment is thoughtful, Sandy is adamant that her spirit is not in those ashes, but right beside you, as she was in life. She says, "I am as alive as I ever was!" Sandy is truly all around you, Carol. She is still at the foot of your bed and around your legs as you cook in the kitchen. Sandy is still hoping to get a treat there!

She disclosed to me the reason she was sent to you and your son. For you, Sandy showed you the unconditional, unwavering love that only a dog can. For your son, Sandy helped him realize some life lessons about love and loss to make him a stronger person. She was here to teach him what true love really means, how to cherish it, and how to live in the present with it. Because of Sandy's influence, your son is beginning to form a deeper understanding of love and death. What a gift Sandy gave!

But the reading did not end there! Amazingly, Sandy sent me the words of a poem she had for you, Carol:

"I am still around you,
I did not go far.
When you look up at night,
I am that star.
First thing in the morning,
You think of me.
I have never left you,
I didn't leave."

Sandy left had me with the memory of the number 12 and was holding up the paw of another dog. She said she had a long and happy life during her time on Earth and could not have asked for more.

As you know, Carol, I had to call you after that! Thank you for confirming that Sandy's pain was, in fact, in her hind legs and spine. I loved hearing the story of how you felt you had "rescued" Sandy, even though you purchased her from a pet store in the mall in Leominster. You kept returning to the mall to visit her there, and each time you asked to hold her. One day you noticed the tag on Sandy's collar exactly matched the date of your father's birthday. He passed when you were just 12!

Thank you, too, Carol, for clarifying what Sandy was referring to when she was holding up the paw of another dog in the vision I had of her. Apparently, this other dog had a bad accident involving his paw and had to be taken to the emergency animal hospital for treatment.

I loved hearing about the time Sandy very nearly saved your life when you had a bad fall. Sandy laid over your body, protecting it, and barked and barked until help arrived. What a good dog!

If my readers are curious if their deceased pets are still around them, here are some common signs to look for:

- You hear their paws padding around the house or running up and downstairs.
- You hear them purring or panting.
- You feel their presence as they curl up on the bed or couch beside you.
- You feel them jump up and actually leave an impression on the bed or seat beside you.

- You catch a glimpse of them in your peripheral vision.
- You have a happy memory of the two of you together.

Readers, know that your pets are with you for a reason. Their love is pure and unconditional. Did you know that your pets that pass on could become spirit guides to you in this life? They can reincarnate as well and go through may lifetimes with you as an ever-faithful companion.

They stay by your side in both life and death and will be waiting for you with wagging tails in Heaven, happy to be together again.

Every night my Great Dane, Sinbad, who is in spirit now, comes and puts his nose on my nose at night to say hello from Heaven. Love never dies.

Cat Calls to Owner from Beyond

Dear Bonnie: My beloved 16-year-old cat Mosey died recently. I am heartbroken over the loss of my furry companion, yet at the same time would like to rescue another cat or kitten to ease my loneliness. Can you contact Mosey on the other side and see if he would be upset, or think he is being "replaced" too soon by another rescue cat? — Norm

Dear Norm: I am so very sorry for the loss of your beloved Mosey! Pets become family members, particularly those that give their love and companionship so freely for so many years.

Please be reassured that Mosey's spirit came to me almost immediately. A soul is a soul, and all sentient beings go to Heaven, regardless of species. Mosey, a multicolored cat, was sitting contentedly on the lap of a woman in a rocking chair in Heaven. Norm, I believe this is your mother. She said to me, "Tell Norm that I have Mosey here with me." She has heard you ask her that very question, and yes, they are together in Heaven.

I know cats can sometimes be aloof, but not Mosey. He is a fabulous communicator! He told me clearly that he would be honored if you were to rescue another shelter cat. Please don't feel guilty for wanting animal companionship, Norm. Mosey even showed me the two kittens, one of which looks like him, that you had visited at the shelter earlier that day.

Thank you, Norm, for sharing your sweet stories of how Mosey would sleep above your head at night, with a protective paw on your face. He did very much have the attitude of a watchdog! Mosey would strut around your home, protecting you. He did love going outside and appreciated it when you would bring him out, under your careful supervision.

Mosey is funny, too. He told me in Heaven he still plays with mice but now he doesn't eat them!

Toward the end of his Earthly life Mosey said his tummy and his paw hurt. Thank you for confirming this with your vet, Norm. Mosey passed when the time was right for him. He felt he had a long, happy, and loving life.

In Heaven Mosey is healthy and happy and having fun outside. Have you felt his spirit jumping on the bed at night, keeping close to you? Mosey reminds us he can never be replaced but would love for you to have a special bond with another cat that needs a loving home. Mosey even volunteered to train the new kitten to be a "watchdog" like he was, and a protective companion with which to share your home.

Norm, as I was communicating with Mosey, your son, Scott, came through. I am sorry for the loss of your son. To me, he appeared as a teenager. In Heaven, your son is happy and with other family members. He's got a great sense of humor, too. He showed me his photograph that you keep on a shelf beside the TV - next to Mosey's! A place of honor, indeed.

I know that Mosey helped you process the grief of losing your son. This was part of his soul contract with you.

Animals are souls as well and have a purpose in this life for each of us. It is their sacred honor to spend their days with us as unconditionally loving companions. It's no mistake or whim when you bring your pet home with you. It's divinely guided. We are all members of God's kingdom and learn from and love each other, regardless of species. Whatever animal you hold near and dear to your heart is an essential element of both of your souls' journeys.

Thank you, Norm, for rescuing these animal souls and making them a part of your life. There are many shelters out there with animals that are looking to spend their years with us, helping us on our soul's journey.

A Pet's Love is Forever

Dear Bonnie: I have a question. I had to put my husky to sleep after 15 years of her being one of my best friends. I have been mumbling to myself and still talking to her like she is still around. Tonight, my son and I went out to look at the snow moon and take a picture. In every picture we took, we noticed that there appear to be white and colored round spots or circles. Could this be an orb? My question is, could my beloved dog show up as an orb? Thanks. — Pete

Dear Pete: First of all, let me say I am so sorry for the passing of your fur baby. Our animals are souls and mean just as much as another soul to us, as they should. Animals that have such a strong bond with us are always here to support us on our journey called life here in the physical world.

Many dogs and cats and all kinds of animals hang around us for a few days after their passing to ensure we will be all right without them. This could be one of the reasons you keep feeling her presence and continuing to talk to her.

As I feel her spirit and blend with her, she starts to tell me about the unique love story the two of you had. Not only did you save her, but she truly saved you as well. There were many stories of love, and she especially wants to call attention to when you first met. Yes, I am blending in with the soul of your husky as she sends me thoughts and images from above.

Animal communication is not my specialty, but it is just as easy to talk to a beloved dog as it is to talk to a dad on the other side. She brings me to a scene when you first met, and she looks into your eyes. She instantly knows that she is the one for you; it seems it took you a little longer.

At the beginning of your journey together and a few times in between, some situations were a little rough on both of you. She tells me school and moving were two of these things. I know as the family grew, so did the love that bound you all together. I see the woman in your life loves her as well, even though there seem to be some obstacles they work out. She shows me she waits at the door to go on long walks. The longer, the better, and she loved the cold and snow.

She hated to leave you behind because you felt more like her child, and regrets having to leave you here without her. After all, she knows you are devastated.

She hears you as she passes, giving her words of comfort about running free and being pain-free, and wants you to hold the knowledge in your heart that she is once again with no pain and jumping fences freely. Keep looking up into the sky and pay attention to the lights and the orbs, because you asked for her to let you know she was okay in the spirit world.

She is trying to show you that although she misses you, she is happy and alive on the other side. So please don't be sad. She asks me to tell you and to let you know she is still at the front door scratching her nails against the wood to go on a walk with you.

Keep going for walks and take her along even though you may not see her; you can still sense her presence. She tells me you have a lot to do yet in this lifetime. Keep doing your best; others depend on you. You have given her the gift of a long and happy life. Your best friend will always be watching, guiding, and protecting you from the other side of life. She tells me you have got this.

So, to answer your question, yes, keep an eye open and watch for her signs as love is always love, and her love will always be with you.

The Story of Zeus and Jesus

Dear Bonnie: I have heard that all dogs go to heaven. Do you believe this to be true? I just lost my family beagle, and I am so distraught. I would like to believe that our beloved fur children know the way over the Rainbow Bridge, but I would like to know your thoughts. — Greg

Dear Greg: I know that our beloved pets and animals are never left behind and are treated like the blessed souls that they are. Let me tell you about a personal story that happened to me. It is a hard story to write about, as it has such a tragic ending, but I feel this story will help to heal a lot of hearts by telling it.

My son was in the Army and needed to leave his dog with my husband and me while he went on special duty. His dog became the baby of the family and very much loved by both of us. Zeus was a big dog but always gentle as he laid at my feet while I watched TV and slept beside my bed at night. Zeus and I became best buddies.

One morning as I got out of bed, I looked to see Zeus sitting up on the floor but with a different kind of expression on his face. I reached over to pat the top of his head, but his expression did not change. I went in to take my shower, thinking it was strange that Zeus did not follow me as I got up to go into the other room. I came out of the shower and continued to my room to get dressed when Zeus became violent and, with his teeth showing, began to lunge full force toward me.

Instantly, the door between us snapped closed, and I did not remember ever pulling the doorknob (hence angels stepping in, as they can if they need to save a life). I was stunned at the way he wanted to attack me. The commotion awoke my husband, and he was able to take control of Zeus. I had gone into another room and was crying when Zeus again bared his teeth.

My husband got Zeus to the veterinarian and told them the story. My son's sweet dog's mind had snapped. I could not make any sense of it. He was now a threat to others and could not be trusted with any humans. My husband returned home alone.

As I went to sleep that evening, a man appeared to me from the spirit world. He was wearing a lab coat and sat on a desk. He assured me I had done nothing wrong, and unfortunately, this sometimes happens.

The next day I was amazed to see Zeus in spirit, walking up and down the hallway. I knew he was in spirit, but he seemed sad, walking with his head down. I could sense the remorse as I called to him, and he came close. I whispered, "I forgive you. It is okay."

I started my day as usual until I received a call from my sister, who also has the gift of clairvoyance. She announced that Zeus was stuck between worlds because he felt he had done something wrong. She told me I needed to sit quietly and send him to the white light.

I had never done anything quite like this, but as I sat and connected to the spirit world, Jesus appeared. He quietly asked me to hand Zeus to him. I saw myself reaching down to pick up Zeus, who was a big dog, but as soon as I picked him up, he turned into a puppy and was handed to Jesus. As soon as he was safely in Jesus' hands, they both were gone. Jesus had come to take Zeus into the light where he belonged.

No soul is ever left behind, and I found out firsthand. I know some of the things I am shown are meant to be shared with others, as I never talk or teach without knowing these things are true.

I still miss Zeus and was so sad to tell my son the news of his beloved pet. But I am happy to say I see him happy and healthy in heaven.

Yes, I believe in the Rainbow Bridge, but I am also glad to know that Jesus takes the time for all those pets that might lose their way of getting there. I hope this story eases the minds of those who love their fur babies as their children.

Pets' Souls are Always Reaching Out to Us

Dear Bonnie: I think my beloved dog Jack is trying to communicate with me from heaven, and I would like to know some ways he might be coming through. Can you give me some tips on what to look for? Jack passed just a few weeks ago, and I was devastated when he became ill. I would feel better if I knew he made it across the Rainbow Bridge. — Pat

Dear Pat: Our animals or babies are souls, and Jack's soul would try to reach out to you in many ways. They want us to know they are happy and at peace with their passing.

When we go on vacation, the first thing we do is to call home to tell our loved ones that we made it to our destination. Our loved ones and fur babies want us to know they are safe and sound.

In the beginning, when they first pass, is when you would receive the most signs that they are trying to get a message to you. During this stage they know you are sad and distraught, and they want you to know that even though they are not in the physical world, they are still very much with you. After they know you are receiving the messages, their visits will become less frequent to let you go through the healing process.

When they come so close to you that you can feel their presence around you is the time when they are visiting you and you have a thought of them, and then the tear slips down your face. It's because their soul has come so close to your soul.

Here are some other ways your pets can show their presence:

- You can hear their paws or their nails on your hardwood floors.
- If your cat wore a bell on her collar, you might hear the bell.
- You hear scratching on the back door like they used to do when they wanted to go out.
- You feel them curled up beside you on the couch or your bed.
- They leave an impression on the cushion next to you showing you they are there.

- You see them in your peripheral vision for a second or two.
- You have a visitation at night in your dreams, and you can feel them with you.

The dream part is my favorite and seems to be the easiest way for your pets to have a visit with you. I know my dogs that are in Heaven will come into my dream time and place their nose on my nose. It's always the best hello from heaven.

If you want to have a visit from your loved one or fur baby, ask before you go to sleep that you receive a visit and that you remember having this joyful time, so in the morning you will know for sure it was a true visit.

Your loved ones never leave you and are always by your side protecting and guiding and still very much watching out for you.

Dream or Visit?

Dear Bonnie: Can you tell me the difference between a dream and a visitation from Heaven? Some nights I am just having an ordinary dream and other nights I feel as though I am actually sitting with my mom at the kitchen table having a cup of tea with her. How do I know what's real? — Thanks, Peggy

Dear Peggy: We actually do dream and have visitations with our loved ones at night. Our loved ones are always trying to get messages to us. These messages are usually based on what's happening in our lives at the moment or maybe they are trying to help us figure something out. The golden hour is usually around 3 a.m. when we are in a deep sleep and then we awaken because our loved ones have drawn near; it brings us back and out of that state of being.

Years ago, I was always waking up at 3 a.m. and I would get up and have a cup of tea. My husband would get up at 4 a.m. to get ready for work and he would say "oh, they woke you up again." Now that I do this work, I still have visits from heaven while I am sleeping, but my mind seems to recognize what's happening and then I can continue to sleep through the night. That is when the veil is the thinnest and communication seems to be easier.

Visitations are actual visits from heaven from our loved ones, guides, and angels. These visitations will seem more real-like. Usually, we can hear the person talking, laughing, and we actually can hear ourselves having a conversation with them. Your loved one would appear in good health and looking happy and often showing us what they are doing in Heaven.

Your loved ones on the other side want you to know that they are at peace and often show us how they are living on the other side. Some are in the homes they built here on earth but now have in Heaven or they might be learning to ski if they always wanted to here on Earth and didn't get the chance. They also want you to know they are looking after you, guiding you whenever you need their help and offering encouragement with your soul's journey.

If you are having dreams that are frightening or not making sense but are leaving you weary, take a look at your bedtime routine. I have clients that come to me and ask, "Why am I dreaming these bad dreams? I think my loved one in Heaven needs me." When I connect to their loved ones, I usually hear that they are watching too much of the scary murder mystery stuff on TV before they are going to bed at night.

Your loved ones will always be positive when they come through because all the petty stuff gets left behind when you enter those pearly gates.

Our minds and thoughts are all energy, so your thoughts are what you bring into your nighttime with you. I know if I want a visit from the angels, I read one of my angel books before I go to sleep. I know if I bring out the check book and the bills before going to bed it's not going to be such a great night's sleep.

If you want a visitation, try doing a meditation, taking out all the thoughts and things that you did from the day and making them disappear, and then your mind will be ready to receive the good stuff and leave out the bad. Want a visitation with a loved one? Try putting their photo under your pillow or wearing a piece of their clothing. I still wear my mom's slippers sometimes.

Visitations from Heaven

Dear Bonnie: How can I tell if I am having a dream about my loved ones or truly having a visitation from them in Heaven versus making things up in my own mind? I feel my parents around me at different times and it always makes me feel safe. Are there some ways I can tell for sure? —Thanks, Dawn

Dear Dawn: Visitations from heaven seem to feel more real and often you can hear your loved ones speaking with you. You might even see a whole scenario going on, almost like you're in a play. If you can see vibrant colors, hear music, and feel a hug from a loved ones, it's probable you are having a visit from Heaven. These visits usually tend to happen when we need a little extra TLC. The spirit world is not some far-off place, and our loved ones are close by, especially when you're feeling down or need that hug.

You can also have a visitation from a pet that you have had a connection with. Many times, during mediumship readings I will see your pets that have passed still around you. That connection never goes away. Recently, I wasn't feeling well myself and just before waking up I saw my Great Dane, Sinbad, and my golden retriever, Captain Jack, sitting at the top of my driveway as though they were guarding my home and standing guard over me like they always did.

I am like you; I was excited they were together and showing me that they were still around me even after years have passed. I felt comforted and safe. If you feel your cat jump on your bed like she always did, say hello, and welcome the visit, as cats often stay close.

During an event I was giving at an inn in New Hampshire, a white horse started following me around the room. This horse, of course, was in the spirit realm, but wanted me to give a message to her owner. I did, and it was such an amazing heartfelt message, the tears were flowing.

Other visitations may include feeling a chill all of a sudden and there is no breeze or actual temperature change. We can sometimes feel the energy of our loved ones when they are in our presence. Have you ever felt a quick chill and you've asked yourself what it was? It might be your loved one coming or going.

Another feeling is actually a feeling of bliss that happens all around you, but for some unknown reason. This feeling almost feels like pure joy has surrounded you and could be your hug from a loved one or an angel as they wrap their heavenly wings around you.

How can you tell if you have been visiting Heaven? We have a cosmic cord that keeps us connected to God and Heaven, and we visit them just like our loved ones visit us. If you have ever been asleep and all of a sudden your whole body starts to jerk, it might be your soul coming back from a visit and you're feeling the coming home part. When I ask my clients if this has ever happened to them more often than not, I get a yes.

When you know you are experiencing a visit, try to stay calm and enjoy the moment. Write down your experience on a piece of paper and try not to think about it too much. Acknowledge that it happened. I am sure there will be more to come. Before you go to sleep at night ask for a visit. It might not happen that first night but don't give up. Your loved ones want to talk to you as much as you want to talk to them.

A Visit from Dad

Dear Bonnie: I was sleeping, and I woke up to the realization that I had one bad dream after another. I have had a lot going on with friends that I work with being kind to my face, but then not so much when they think I can't see or hear them. It's so competitive at my job and there is so much pressure that it's affecting my sleep time. Any advice? Thanks, Allison

Dear Allison: This week I also found myself paying too much attention to what others are doing with their lives and how successful they all appear to be. I took those thoughts and feelings with me when it was time to go to sleep, only to have them follow me through the night. Now, I know that I have heard the voice of God telling me to put my blinders on and only pay attention to myself and what I am doing and the reasons I do things as a medium. I am still human, though, and I am sure, like me, you can find yourself wondering when our time is.

Well, let me tell you what happens when you bring fear and worry into your sleep time. Bad dreams can happen, like snakes are chasing me or I see myself flying over the mountains and fields to stay away from the harshness we all face on Earth. Your dreams might be different, but needless to say, they are not what we want to be dreaming.

This particular night the spirit world stepped in, and I saw the face of my father, who passed two years ago. I can and do see the spiritual world all the time, but this was different. My father's face and the way he was looking at me with his blue eyes was something special. His face was so close to mine, I could see the pores in his skin.

I then heard the words outside of my head telling me, "Don't be fooled!" kind of like that saying, "All that glitters is not gold." I know my father saw that I was upset and that my feelings were hurt by people who don't care or know me well. I was amazed at the energy it must have taken him to appear so close with me, bringing with him a message to soothe my soul. The spirit world amazes me over and over again, not to mention the love of a parent on the other side.

It's our lesson in life to surround ourselves with people who genuinely care and want the best for us, and to remove those from our lives who don't. It's okay to be picky when it comes to whose energy is affecting your energy. Protect yourself as you surround yourself in God's white light of protection.

Before going to bed, make sure you take time to relax or meditate before you try to fall off into sleep. God has told me it's your thoughts that create your dream time. If you want a visit from a loved one during the night, before falling asleep ask for a visit from them that you will remember in the morning.

All that glitters is not gold. Don't be fooled! We all are in this together. So, shine your light and try not to let others shine their light into your eyes.

Celebrity Visits

Dear Bonnie: Have you ever had a celebrity visit or has a celebrity ever come through while you were giving a message to a client? — Sonya

Dear Sonya: I have never attempted to talk to a celebrity just because I wanted to see if I could. However, I have had celebrity visits. I will share with you some of them. I seem to have celebrities who were a little before my time but that I do know about or have seen in old movies, some coming to share details with me. I did not ask; they just appeared to have answers to questions I have had in my real life.

One night, I went to sleep thinking about how I wanted my hair to be styled and colored. I was going to ask my hairstylist, as I had an appointment the next morning, and during the night I awoke to see Marilyn Monroe before me. She did not say anything, but I knew she was showing me her hair. It was short, stylish, and very blond, and I knew she was trying to get that color to me in hopes it would help me with my hair decisions.

The next morning, I went to my stylist and, lo and behold, she had a picture of Marilyn Monroe next to her station. I took her advice, and I still have that same blond hair to this day. You might ask yourself why Marilyn Monroe would care about my hair. I do not know that for certain, but I do know a soul is a soul. She had a sweet presence about her, and I think she thought her color would look good on me.

Visits do not have to be life-changing, but always seem to be helpful. Now, would I call up and ask Marilyn Monroe to have a chat with me? No, I would not. But I sure liked seeing her and receiving her advice on my beauty choices.

Another celebrity visit came from Bing Crosby. It was around Christmas time, and I have his Christmas CDs and was listening to them one afternoon. That evening, as I went to bed, I had the question in my mind about a legal matter that was taking place and when I would be getting notice of the outcome.

That night Bing appeared to me. He nodded his head as if to say, "Hello," put on his fedora and said, "March 15th." That was it. He left me with a date that, in the morning, I remembered very clearly. A letter came on that exact day, letting me know what the outcome was on that matter. Wow!

What does that prove? The spirit world knows what is going to happen before we do, and Bing was on the money with that one. Even I was amazed at the accuracy of that date, because I live in a small town, and we never know when our mail is coming, as sometimes it takes longer than average.

Another time, while driving to work, very much awake this time, Robin Williams spoke to me like he was sitting next to me riding shotgun. It was just after his tragic passing, and I could hear his voice so clearly. I loved watching all his TV shows and movies and had just watched a video he had made a week before.

His tragic passing had taken me by surprise, as he always looked so happy. Robin, however, had a request to deliver a message to someone, and we chatted for a few minutes, and I told him I probably would not be able to reach this person for a few reasons. Imagine someone calling you out of the blue and telling you they have a message for you.

He understood and, even though I felt terrible that I could not help, he reassured me it was okay. Then he was gone, and once again I was alone in my car, driving to work. These stories go to show that we are all one and always connected on some level, on Earth as in Heaven, although in Heaven we get to see the bigger picture of why some things work out and others do not. Our egos do not hold us, and we are of pure light.

What I have learned from these experiences and why I am sharing them with you is because it is not the job that you hold here on Earth that makes you who you are, but the love in your heart that makes you a good person, the person who might give a stranger some help with her hair or the exact date of an occasion that will take place, taking away worry from someone you have never met.

It might even be asking for help from someone who doesn't know, but being able to see the compassion in someone's heart that they might be able to help you.

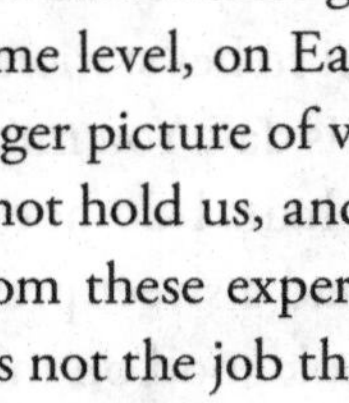

You Have Always Had the Power

Dear Bonnie: With all that is going on in our world at this time, are there any messages from the spiritual world that would be comforting at this time? Have you received any guidance or knowledge? — Robert

Dear Robert: I have been asked this a lot in the past month, if I knew if there was some big message coming down from Heaven, and I can only share with you my thoughts and my opinions that I have gathered.

When the virus started emerging and we were told to become aware and start distancing ourselves, I said out loud, "God is giving us a timeout," only to hear the words as they came back to me. "I have not done this. I love my children," He answered back.

I was startled as I listened and then felt terrible for even having the thought that God would ever wish this on us for any reason. I quickly apologized by sending that thought back to Heaven and said, "Of course, you would not wish this on us."

I also loved the idea of having a couple of weeks off and staying in my home until I realized I was selfish with not acknowledging that people were dying. It's a sad day for us all any way you look at it. Did I need a couple of weeks off to give my soul and body a break from the 9-to-5? That could have been a choice I chose for myself without an epidemic going on.

What I have learned these last few weeks is that people have kind and amazing souls and that we are all stronger than we think we are, but most importantly, that everyone in Heaven is with us even stronger in our times of need.

Now, I know lots of people were given a heads-up that "we are here" before this started, and that came with hearing and seeing the spirit world more clearly than ever. I have heard from people all over our country in emails that they have shared with me their incredible stories of communication with loved ones in dreams or signs from Heaven.

I know in my heart and soul that we will never be the same after experiencing this time in our lives. I believe we will never again take for granted the love that permeates in our hearts for our family and friends, and for those we have never met, that we will view all the love and freedom as beautiful connections to humankind and our nation.

Look deep into your soul and ask yourself, "What am I learning from having this experience on Earth at this time? What can I do to help make my family and others feel safe, wanted, and protected?"

I channeled a message from Heaven and heard, "You are loved, and in this time, there are two choices: Find the faith and compassion within your heart and use that to help others in some way or get caught up in your head and let fear diminish all you could be doing at this time to help others and yourself. The choice is yours. Turn inside of yourself and reconnect with your soul as this is the time for you to see what matters the most to you and your soul's journey."

That was the message, short but sweet and to the point. God gives you free will and does not take that away. I ask you all to take that in-depth look within yourself to find what your soul was meant to do in this lifetime and to see if you are on the course that was always there before you. You have always had the power.

Living a Spiritual Life

Dear Bonnie: I'm trying to become more spiritual about the way I react to others and how I think about life, but every time I think I'm becoming the person I want to be it seems to go down the drain. Any suggestions on how I can overcome this? — Jen

Dear Jen: It's not the easiest thing in the world, learning to adjust to any adversities that pop up in our lives. It's going to happen to even the most spiritual people on the planet.

You seem to have it all figured out. Do unto others as you would have them do to you. Live your life with intention and have a beautiful and peaceful soul. You know you're a good person who tries to treat others with respect and without judging. You give to charities, and you smile at everyone you meet on the street or in the grocery store. You pay attention to the feelings of friends and family and even people you don't know very well.

You pray and meditate, and everything seems to be on an even keel, and then what happens? A life-changing experience shakes your world, an experience you didn't see coming, the loss of a loved one or a sickness in the family. You get laid off from a job you love. You lose your best friend, or your marriage falls apart. It has happened to all of us.

When you're doing your very best with everything you put out to the world, you start to wonder why. Why would this happen to me? What did I do to deserve this? It's like the song, "Why Me, Lord?" It's not easy trying to live a more spiritual life, but I can tell you, in the end it will pay off. Troubles and tribulations happen for a reason. Sometimes we can't see the how or why, and we may never find out. I can tell you, though, that how we react to a situation or problem when it does arise can be a great test of who we really are. They are lessons to be learned so our soul can grow to be perfect and expand in every way.

Things sometimes happen so that we too can understand what it feels like when difficulties happen to others. We will live a life having more sympathy or compassion for others with similar problems. The sooner we handle situations with an open mind and ask the question, "What am I to learn?" the faster the problem or situation can move away from us.

After my mom passed, my siblings and I fell apart from each other, something I never thought would happen, and I sought the answers as to why. Clients started coming in for readings who had the same situation happening to them, and I knew then how to counsel them with a greater sympathy that I probably would not have felt as deeply if I hadn't been going through the same thing myself. I looked to heaven and said, "I get it. I am not alone."

When you feel like something is happening just to you, believe me, it's not. I have learned firsthand that spirits know what you are going through, and they are trying their very best to shine a light on the situations that we must endure, but they cannot take away the lesson.

If you do not handle a situation with grace and receive the lesson, it will come back to you time and time again until you have grown stronger, until no one has the power to take you away from that feeling of peace. That's when you truly know you are living a spiritual life, when you have faith in God that you are being cared for.

We will not live a complete life of contentment until we return home to Heaven. This is our schoolroom, and we are here to learn. It's a journey, what we signed up for before we came down on Earth to live. We picked our family, friends, and lessons beforehand. It's hard to imagine that, but we did. We can't control our situations, but we can control our actions.

Next time you can show your bright light to others by handling yourself with grace and love, you will feel the feeling of contentment, knowing that you have made the right choice for you. Life is full of disappointments, but remember the old saying, "When one door closes, another will open." Keep living a spiritually filled life. It's not just for you but for everyone who can see it shining brightly. Blessings.

How to Foster Change

Dear Bonnie: I seem to go through each day in a fog of too many things to do with so little time. Do you have any tips to foster change? — Betty

Dear Betty: This is a question that comes up quite often when I am with clients who want to know the secret of living a happy, spiritually filled life. I, for one, understand the challenges of getting everything done that we want to achieve, and I can tell you it's all about finding balance. We need a plan to have a happy life, one that is filled with family, friendships, a job we love, and a life that can be lived with no regrets.

Sounds like a lot to ask for, you say. But what if we don't have a plan? There are only so many hours in a day and only so many days in our life. When we are young, our life has a different way of appearing than when we start to get into our 50s and 60s. There are different questions we are faced with, not the least of which is, "Are we living our best life now?"

I would ask you to break down time by making a plan for the very best possible day that you can. If we don't make plans or give ourselves goals, we can find ourselves letting life go by and not really achieving the happiness that is meant to be ours.

God wants us to live life to its fullest while enjoying our time on Earth. So many things can get in the way of what is truly important. Are you in a job you hate but you like the money? Do you wish you were in better physical shape, but you don't watch what you're eating or take the time to exercise?

Are you spending enough time with family and friends, and sharing special moments and memories with the ones you love? Life is about making choices and then following a plan. How disciplined you are with your time makes all the difference in the world. I know it's not easy, but it takes action, not just wishing, to make something happen.

If you want to be skinny, you need to eat healthy, low-fat foods and exercise. There is just no other way. You want to write a book? It takes the discipline of sitting down and starting to write and the patience and time to get it finished. If you need education for a new job you would like to have, start by taking one course at a time if you need to. It's just following a plan for your life, one day at a time.

When you reach the end of your earthly journey, what do you think are going to be the things that will count as most important; the money you earned or the family that means so much to you? We all need to earn a living, but ask yourself, "Am I living my best life now?"

Find ways of planning your days so it's not just week after week of "going through the motions." Set goals of what is important to you and do your best to achieve them. Make a list and set your intention for your day. If your list has ten things on it and you only accomplish four of them, don't beat yourself up. Instead, be thankful for what you did accomplish, that you set your goals, and pick up where you left off the following day.

It's the shout-out to the universe that you have goals and are doing your best. When you set that intention, it gives the universe permission to step in and help you to achieve your goal. It's like having cheerleaders in Heaven who want to see you meet your goals!

Just remember to have fun. Sometimes we need to schedule that in also. It's your life. Make it work for you and not the other way around.

How do You See Your Life?

In 10th grade, my high-school history teacher had us sit and write our obituary. We were so young and had not really started to live life. Why would he ask us to do this, you say? He wanted to show us how our life could look in the end. How do you want others to see you when you're ready to leave this Earth? I am sure we all looked a little perplexed staring up at him.

He told us many great people in history have done amazing things and have amazing stories of how they accomplished their goals in their lifetime. My teacher wanted us to envision what we could do with the time we had here. He wasn't trying to scare us; more so he wanted us to take a good, long look into the future, to truly see what we could manifest while having the best life possible for ourselves and making a difference in someone else's life or lives, to truly live a life worth living.

We sat in class and tried to write the best story of how our lives would unfold. I remember very clearly envisioning a happy marriage and children and having a happy future. In addition to that, I am not sure what I wrote, but I do know it stuck with me this whole time.

In fact, every time I have accomplished a new goal or gone to places I've always wanted to go, I imagine it written down in my obituary. Sounds kind of eerie, you say, but really, it's about living a fulfilled life and being proud of the life you are living.

What do you want others to remember about you? Ask this question as you move forward. What do you want to be remembered for? I have had a happy marriage and family, for which I am so grateful, something I never take for granted.

Think of your obituary as a vision board. What is your calling? How do you want to fulfill your soul's calling? Is work just a paycheck to you or is your work helping others in some way?

Are you happy as you look back at where you've been and how far you've gotten? Are your goals coming to fruition or have you let them sit on the sideline, waiting for someone to step in and take action?

This is your time to write your obituary. If you don't like that idea, sit, and write down the life's plan you have for yourself. We only have so much time here. With a little planning it can be filled with love, compassion, and fulfilled dreams.

When you write down what you truly desire it gives the universe permission to step in and help with your plans. How do you want to be remembered? More importantly, what do you want for your life?

Go big. Dream big. What can it hurt?

Make Every Day Meaningful

Dear Bonnie: Sometimes I feel as though I am just going through the steps of life. like it's this big race and everything seems to keep going around and around with nothing new happening. It's not what I imagined my life would be, and I never seem to be enough. — Cooper

Dear Cooper: I do know how you feel. Life can be so exciting at times, and at other times it seems everything is the same day after day, almost like that movie "Groundhog Day" where the guy keeps waking up to the same day over and over again.

I think these are the times when we need to start dreaming about how we would like our life to be and begin to imagine ourselves living the dream we had when we were young, not being afraid or worried about what might happen, a time when we used our imaginations and believed we could be whatever we wanted, the dreams of our younger soul and why we chose to come down to explore this time on Earth.

We can get stuck in a rut if we are not careful, especially when we see our lives not turning out exactly as we imagined they would, each time accepting disappointment instead of seeing it as an opportunity. When we see challenges as opportunities to grow, we can move away from the problem or frustration with new vigor, almost like taking on a new assignment and figuring out how to make lemons into lemonade.

We think we need to follow the rules that society has set for us: the pressure to look like that model on the front cover of the magazine. One gym puts down another and the people in it to gain customers for themselves. Living in a world in which knocking down the dreams of others seems to be okay, it's easy to get caught up in the negativity that surrounds us and makes us look less than perfect.

If you have faith that everything is happening for a greater reason and things may not look like they are supposed to, every decision you make is just a choice that is yours to make because you have God's free will. If you embrace the knowledge that you are perfect just the way you are and dream big for yourself, then you can see the world from a different point of view: just a classroom, not where your soul lives.

Let the soul of that little girl or boy within you explore and learn, dance, and feel, be one with yourself and others. Love is the reason you have stepped into this life. You have the choice of waking up each morning feeling like it's "Groundhog Day" or jumping out of bed with vigor and asking yourself what new adventures will come today.

I'm not saying it's easy, but I am saying it's a decision. So have faith, say a prayer, and ask for help from above, then enjoy your day, because one day of our life that isn't meaningful in some way seems wasted when it could have been amazing.

This poem came to me a few weeks ago. I think it fits nicely.

Free

Free to be me
To watch the sunrise
In the morning
To see the glow of happiness
On a child's face
To hear the birds
As they swoop down to visit
Free to see the beauty
In all living things
To accept all things
Are possible
And nothing is a given
But everything is
A gift
Free to be me

God's Guidance

Dear Bonnie: I find it hard living in today's society where no one seems happy anymore. The people I encounter don't seem to be interested in anything I have to say or even smiling back if I do make the effort. I want to live a happy life, but it almost seems impossible in today's world. Do you have any suggestions? — Ari

Dear Ari: I know it seems hard to live a life filled with gratitude, but it does seem to help if you put your best foot forward. We can only take responsibility for our own actions and not the actions of others.

We can start each day by taking a moment to thank God for the little things as well as the big events that happen in our lives. Living a life of gratitude can be demanding for sure, but when you make the effort, it does pay off.

Last week, on my cruise to the Caribbean, I took the chance to face one of my fears of riding a horse. I grew up with horses, and I do love them but have had some pretty terrifying moments when riding. I decided I was going to try again on an excursion.

The last time I rode was on my pony Sonny. He was a beautiful painted pony but young and had his own ideas. We started on a ride that ended with me being pulled through the woods. As Sonny looked down, he gazed into a puddle, seeing his own shadow, and becoming frightened. He bolted with me and off we went.

I managed to bring him to a halt just a few yards away from a huge hole that surely would have swallowed us up. I was only 12, and that was the start of my riding adventures. Later, I was riding, and the saddle became loose, and I ended underneath the stomach of my pony. Angels were very much with me that day, as Sonny became perfectly still and did not trample me. It's like an angel held his reins as I gently fell to the ground.

So, on this day, I decided to put these memories to rest. It didn't entirely turn out as I imagined, almost instantly becoming overwhelmed with anxiety as I climbed up on a horse named Ginger. She immediately knew I was hesitant and started misbehaving, putting her head down and bucking. That was enough for me; I wanted off. Then a guide came around and took the reins, telling me I was okay and that he was going to help me. I had to take a deep breath and ground myself.

My guide stayed close, and as we rode along the path, I started to connect with my dad in Heaven, apologizing for having this fear. He loved his horses and was an avid rider. I see him in Heaven riding his childhood horse Shaggy. I heard him in my mind saying, "Just because I like something doesn't mean you have to like it."

A little while later, another guide came strolling up on his painted pinto horse, which looked just like my pony, and asked me if I'd like to ride his horse. I thought that was so planned out by spirit, I started to smile. Spirit knows everything, and coming to the end of the ride I felt grateful for my guides' patience and thoughtfulness.

I was also grateful as I got off my horse that day and put my feet back on solid ground. It's the small things in life. I took a moment to thank everyone here and in Heaven for watching out for me.

You don't need to go on a cruise to find the good in people, as good people are all around the world. Try to look for the bright light even when it's not so easy to do.

Listen to what God once said to me: "Have no expectations of anyone and be pleasingly surprised by everyone. So just for today find the gratitude and feel the love. As you give you shall receive."

Find your soul group by becoming involved in the things you like to do. Find support and happiness by making the decision to appreciate the people who come into your life and accepting them as they are. The rest will follow.

Have a Grateful Heart and Watch the Blessings Flow

Dear Bonnie: Is there a way to build spiritual growth? Some days I feel more connected to source than other days. When I do feel connected, I know I feel much happier inside and less worried. — Russ

Dear Russ: It is hard to be positive and feel close to God and the spirit world all the time, and part of that is because we live in the physical world where there are jobs to do and bills to pay and lessons to learn. But there are some tips I can pass on that have helped me.

First, I always like to start my morning by saying a little prayer and asking God for his blessings for a healthy, happy, and prosperous day. I feel it sets the tone for my day. Believe it or not, when I get up and start rushing around and forget my little prayer, my day doesn't seem to go as well.

In the shower, you can add to that prayer with an affirmation: "Healthy am I, happy am I, holy am I." Say that three times and end with "and so it is." The water from your shower is taking any old energy off of you and giving you new energy to start your day.

We have an increase in our spiritual growth when we are in alignment with our mind, body, and soul. When we are aligned, our day and life seem to be in harmony, and everything seems to flow in a natural state of ease.

Being grateful for what you have in your life now helps. You can see things in two ways. Your glass can appear to be half empty or half full. There are always two ways of looking at everything that is going on in your life at this moment. I am not saying that the world doesn't look scary out there from time to time; it certainly does if you are growing in one or more areas of your life. Taking chances for growth can be daunting if you are not trusting that the universe has your back.

Before moving on to the next step in your life, be grateful for all the blessings you do have at this moment in time. Don't miss out on the gifts that have been given to you and try to look at the big picture while also looking back at how far you have come.

When you realize what you have in this moment and don't focus on what you do not have, your heart can open to receiving the abundance and connection you are searching for. Take the time to sit and reflex on all the positives that are going on in your life. Sometimes we are waiting for that one thing we hope to come to fruition, and we miss all the joyous situations and love that is already surrounding us.

Have a grateful heart, and watch the blessings start to pour into your life. Be open to all that God and the angels want for you and be open to receiving them. Start writing down the blessings that are coming your way each day. It only takes five minutes of your lunchtime to make a list. Don't leave out the small stuff, as they are blessings also. Your dog waiting for you at the door each night with a kiss for you might seem like a small blessing, but those blessings add up to a fulfilling life.

To be in alignment with God and your heart, nurture your mind, body, and soul. Choose to have a positive attitude, a grateful heart, and loving thoughts throughout your day. Look after your physical body by what you are feeding it. Take great care of your soul and do something spiritual every day.

This is your life — make it a good one. Don't get caught up in what everyone else is doing. Focus on what is important to you and stay in the moment. Have a vision for your life, but don't rush your life trying to get there. Your blessings will come to you if you do your part.

Know that everyone up above is rooting and praying for you to have the life you want and dream about.

How to Stay Positive

Dear Bonnie: With all the recent news about what is going on in our world today, do you have any spiritual ways to keep our thoughts and feelings grounded and not all over the place? I know you say not to be fear-based, and I am trying to stay positive. — Bobbi

Dear Bobbi: Every day can be a scary day if that's what we let our thoughts lead us to. It is the right thing to be cautious in times of crisis, but there are some things we can do to stay positive even in times of tragedy or when we are fearful.

Begin each day by giving the world, your family and yourself a blessing. Prayers are heard, and thoughts are energy. By starting with a positive affirmation or saying a prayer or blessing, you are beginning your day with hope in your heart.

Maybe you are blessed with a family you can count on or a beautiful grandbaby or a best friend who you can tell all your deepest secrets and know that they are safe.

Start with remembering all the blessings that have been bestowed to you. Focus on the positive as it will automatically push the negative thoughts away.

Come up with a word or phrase that can help you stay focused when a negative or scary thought comes into your head. These words can be short like, joy, peace, love, patience, humanity, gratitude, or a longer phrase like, "Please bless us all with a miracle."

Positive words are empowering, and they can help you stay soul-centered. Those positive words are felt deep inside your soul, and as you think of the task at hand for the day, your soul will remain in alignment with the vibrations of positivity.

Negative thoughts will bring your vibration down and positive thoughts raise your vibration. Practice raising your vibration during the day by taking one task at a time and adding a positive spin to it. There are many ways to increase your vibration, and when doing so, you are aligning your chakras, which are your main energy centers in the body. When you keep your chakras running as they are supposed to run and in alignment, your body has a healthier, happier approach to living.

Raise your vibration by eating healthy, colorful fruits and vegetables. While making the bed or working out, play some music that gets your energy going and makes you feel like dancing. Dancing and exercising greatly improve your state of being by moving your body and putting a smile on your face. Watch a funny movie, your favorite comedian, or a funny show on TV.

Raising your vibration is about doing the things that bring you enjoyment and that are fun. We each must do our part when it comes to our happiness. Have faith and trust that we do not always know what is going on in the big picture of life.

Accompanying the column is a sketch of an angel and a little saying I wrote for Facebook this weekend. I hope you enjoy her. Please give her a name.

"I give you an Angel to keep by your side.
She is here for all times,
Good times or bad times she won't leave your side.
Make her your own personal guide.
As she protects you and guides you from Heaven above,
God sends his angels, so you know you are loved.
Protecting, guiding, and shining their light
Angels watch over you all day and all night."

Hope is in the Middle

Dear Bonnie: I find myself always waiting for the next best thing in life. I know that to live a spiritually filled life I need to be mindful of each day. However, I can't seem to find the joy I am looking for because I want to know what the future is. I know a psychic reading can sometimes show you the before, middle and end, and I guess I am always focused on the end. Any suggestions? — Abigail

Dear Abigail: I always go back to a movie I saw years ago called "Hope Floats." There is a part in the movie where Sandra Bullock's character, Birdee Pruitt, quotes her mother. "Beginnings are scary, endings are usually sad, but it's the middle that counts the most. Try to remember that when you find yourself at a new beginning. Just give hope a chance to float up."

I often use this saying in my own life. Beginnings are sometimes scary because we have a fear of the unknown or a fear of doing something for the first time. Even that first kiss might have been a little scary, or the first day on the job, or the first day of school. Scary, but if we don't take those first steps, we might have missed out on many great things.

Then there are endings, and endings can be sad for a lot of reasons; when we know or feel we are losing something we might never have the opportunity again to do, or the ending of a person's life where the ending seems so definite. But endings are a must for many reasons, even though they are sometimes painful.

Endings need to happen for growth in our life. This is where the growth of our soul expands with compassion and sympathy for things and people that are no longer going to be a part of our journey.

In the middle of our journey is where the magic is happening, even though we might not be aware of what is happening behind the scenes. It is at this stage of life that we need to trust. Trust that God and the higher powers know more than we do and are trying to get us to stay on our soul's journey and at the same time give us our free will to decide.

Trust and have faith that our future will look and feel just the way we imagine it will turn out. However, if we rush through until the end to the future, are we not missing the most important part, the middle? The middle is where hope, trust, and faith lie within us. We are not meant to know everything, as that would not let us decide our own life choices.

Enjoy the middle by taking one day at a time and doing your best with where you are. Focus on all the little things that can seem insignificant at the time but may very well turn out to be important when we look back. A psychic reading is an excellent way for a person to receive some guidance.

It can point out where you have been, what's happening now in your life, and maybe show you an idea of what the future might hold for you, but never to determine it for you. Never give anyone that power, because this is your life, and if you wait long enough, hope floats, and you will not want to miss it. Have faith and trust that you are right where you need to be.

Gifts to Share

Dear Bonnie: What would you say if I told you I had lost my passion for life? I thought I knew exactly what I wanted to do in life and how to bring that passion to life by creating my business, but it all seems humdrum to me now. How do I get that passion back and help others with my gifts? I thought I was being called to help others, but I feel burnt out. — Claire

Dear Claire: I do believe we all have a calling in our lives and certain gifts to share when we arrive here in this lifetime. I believe God has given us these gifts to share and to be of service to others.

Let me share my experience with you. I know I was called to help others with my gift of mediumship, but after ten years of doing this work, I felt burnt out as well. I didn't even notice what was happening until I knew I had to take some time off. The need to have some time off was overwhelming, and I knew when talking to clients over the phone that I wasn't feeling or sounding like myself; something was missing.

The best decision I made was to dig deep and sit in meditation to get back to the root of why I was so excited when I started out as a medium in the first place. Soon I realized I had stopped doing some of the things that soothed and ignited my soul. It's all about your soul's journey.

Doing for others is meaningful and fulfilling, but if you are not feeding your soul, the well becomes dry. That's what happened to me. Taking the time to understand why I was not truly happy and excited to do what I loved caused me to look deep down and ask myself what had happened along the way.

With meditation and listening to my inner voice, I realized I was not feeding my own soul with the things that brought me happiness. If we are not happy within ourselves, how can we offer the very best of ourselves to others? I took the time I needed to ask myself what I was missing. Two things came to my heart when I asked, and they will be different for everyone. I found I was missing joy and the feeling I get when filling myself with what fulfills me, which is connecting to God and source energy.

I would ask you to sit in the quiet and ask yourself and your soul, what am I missing? I can tell you that after a few weeks of being committed to filling my soul's needs my passion came back, and happiness came along with it. My attitude and the peace that fills my own soul shine brightly once again. Take the time you need for yourself.

Finding Joy after Loss

Dear Bonnie: My best friend of 30 years passed away recently. Since she died, I have felt a lack of joy or enthusiasm for the things I normally enjoy. My friend and I were constant companions, and we had fun things planned every weekend. Now that she is gone, I feel drained and have no energy. There is no enjoyment when I do the things we used to do together. I know you say we are made of energy. Can you give me some tips on how to feel energetic and joyful again? — Carla

Dear Carla: I am so sorry to hear of your best friend's passing. Please know she is in a beautiful place, and death is hard only for the living. Before I give advice on how to raise your energetic vibration allow me to say that your sadness is a normal part of the grieving process. If it becomes more of a depression than a sadness over your friend's passing, please see your doctor for help. We are here to enjoy life, and to do that we must put our health first.

It's hard losing anyone in our lives, but even harder when they were such a big part of your social circle. Activities that used to seem fun now can feel empty without your companion. We do need to find a way to return to our natural joyful state, not only for ourselves but also so that we may help others in our lives.

Carla, within each of us is a well of energy, which comes up from the Earth through our feet and then branches out throughout our body. Physical energy and emotional joy are closely tied. It's important to keep that well of energy replenished so that we do not become depleted.

Because we receive energy from the Earth, nature is very therapeutic. Do you garden? Get out and dig. Plant some flowers or a tree in her memory. Now that we're close to autumn, you can plant bulbs that will bloom in the spring. It's something for you both to look forward to. Ask her to join you, and as you garden, you can reminisce in your mind over the wonderful experiences you shared.

Did you enjoy going to the beach with her? Take a reflective walk along the shore and maybe collect seashells or sea glass. Look at the shape of what you collect. There may be a message there from her to you! There are lots of fall fairs and outdoor antiques shows happening now, too. Why not check them out?

Don't be surprised if the person in front of you in line at the farmer's market has her mannerisms or you find an item that looks exactly like something she used to own at the antiques show. These are her "hellos" from Heaven to you.

Or, how about the movies? Get a popcorn large enough to share and be sure to reserve the seat beside you for her. Pay attention to the previews or catchphrases throughout the movie. She'll be trying to communicate to you in whatever way she can. Remember, only physical death exists. Her energy and telepathic thoughts will always accompany you. She is still your best friend, only now without her physical body.

Remember, we have an obligation, not only to ourselves but to others, to heal and reclaim our God-given joy. Ask yourself, "What do I need to do to feel like my old self again?"

Affirmations can be a powerful tool to reclaim joy. When you take your shower in the morning, say to yourself, "Healthy am I. Holy am I. Happy am I!" You'll find that positivity will build each day until, in fact, you do feel better. If you are a religious person, you could pray to God to restore your joy.

Because we receive energy from the Earth, try to eat natural, whole foods rather than those with refined sugar, caffeine, and bleached grains (like white bread). Raw foods in particular are especially nutritious as they come directly from Mother Nature and are not processed in any way.

Please try to create beautiful, clean surroundings for yourself as well. Deep-clean your home as much as you are able and clear off any clutter. Light a candle in memory of your friend. Roll up your sleeves and tackle those piles of mail or sink full of dishes. It'll get you physically moving, which boosts your vibration and mood. Plus, a pretty, sparkling, clean home welcomes positive energy.

Lastly, remember to watch your thoughts. Thoughts become things, and we don't want your grief to build into a true depression. It's okay to be sad, but don't linger. If you think, I'll never have a friend like that again, replace that thought with something constructive like, what can I do in her honor today? When you get coffee today, buy the person behind you in line a cup, too. Who knows? You might make a new friend ... one that she sent to comfort you.

Making Changes

Dear Bonnie: I would like to make some changes this year, but I am not sure how to go about it. I would like to start creating a more meaningful way of living. I want to bring in more joy and less stress. Can you offer a spiritual perspective on how to do that? — Sydney

Dear Sydney: It is not easy to make life-changing decisions, but knowing what you need or want is the biggest step. Some people go through their whole life without a plan or destination of where they want to go or who they want to be in this world. It is like taking a road trip without a map.

Living day by day and not setting goals for your life is like letting someone do the driving and not being in control of where you will end up. Setting goals and making plans puts you in the driver's seat and not on an endless ride without a map. Unless you take the time to stop and think about your life and what you want to accomplish, your life can seem like an ongoing movie with no plot.

Think about what means the most to you currently. Is it free time? Career? Family? Schooling? You get the idea. Then ask yourself, what do I need to do to make this happen? Just taking that first step is an accomplishment and a way to bring something to the light of day.

Once you focus your attention on what you want to achieve, the universe will be able to help you put your plans into action. Everything is energy. Your thoughts are energy, and when you begin to turn your energy into achieving this desire, and your thoughts are focused, your energy will not be scattered. Focusing on your desire will help you to manifest what you want to come to fruition. Nothing gets accomplished unless there is a thought and then action behind that thought.

You choose to edit the script of your life at any time. If your wants are different from your needs, roadblocks might pop up out of nowhere. If your plan has many ups and downs, take time to see what is not working and what is working. From there, you will be able to see the map more clearly.

When things are not going your way as you have planned it, it might be the universe giving you a heads up by putting that block in your path. There are always two roads to travel, and the universe has your back and tries to send you down the right path.

There is always divine guidance when you choose your plan. Have patience, compassion with yourself, and follow the plan and your map as best you can. The biggest mistake people make is to make a goal for themselves and then forget that same goal a week later. We are all human, and life happens, so make sure to write down what you hope to accomplish and make that map of what you wish for your life. You can review or edit your plans for your destination at any time. Only then will you be able to clear out what is not serving you or your greater self.

Life goes by fast, so have a plan that makes you feel fulfilled and satisfied. At the end of your life, you do not want to have a regret because you did not take the time to draw a map to where you wanted to end up on your trip called life.

A Christmas Message

Dear Bonnie: This time of the year is so hard. Missing someone in Heaven has me in such pain. I do not feel like celebrating Christmas or even putting up a tree. I do not know how others deal with not having someone to celebrate with, but I keep crying. Can you offer some advice? — Charlotte

Dear Charlotte: As a full-time, medium-giving messenger from your loved ones in Heaven, I recognize this time of the year is the hardest for many.

Last week, a woman came in wanting to speak to her mother, who had passed away less than a month ago. As I started to connect with her mom in spirit, her mom brought me through a sad scene, sending me pictures in my mind of her daughter's bare Christmas tree. As I relayed to her daughter, who was sitting across from me, I saw her well up with tears. She told me she had not been able to decorate the tree. It has been sitting there bare.

Then the mom showed me her daughter's hand placing an ornament on the tree. She told me this was a special ornament in honor of her memory. As I relayed that to her daughter, she replied, "Mom's so right. My friends came over and put some decorations on the tree just last night because I could not do it, and after they left, I got out a special ornament that says 'Mom' and hung that one bulb myself."

You see, moms and dads on the higher side of life know what you did last night. They know your thoughts, your wishes, and even how you are missing them and what ways you are honoring them.

The mom then brought my hand up to the necklace that I wear, a cross, in honor of my mom. It's the last thing she wore for jewelry, and she handed it to me. I now wear it every day in honor of her.

As I relayed the message with my hand around my throat placed on the cross, the woman showed me her necklace that her daughters had given her the previous night in memory of her mom, their grandmother.

Messages don't need to be so evidential that a medium needs to give an address and age, but they need to touch the person's soul. It's all about the love we have shared.

As the woman stood up, she said, "I am sorry I was such a crybaby." My reply was, "When our loved ones come close, it is meant for healing, and releasing tears is a way to do that. So, it's okay to be sad, but then it's okay to be happy also."

Here is a little something that came to me in my dream time:

"I know you are missing me.
I know because I miss you, too.
When you think of me this Christmas,
I will be thinking of you, too.
I know it won't be easy.
I see your tears.
I know it won't be quite the same
As in the other years.
When you think of me this Christmas,
You honor all our love.
All the years of joy and fun,
It can never be undone.
Nothing can break our bond or love
That we have for each other.
When you think of me this Christmas,
Try to remember
The stories of Christmases past.
Do not be afraid to laugh and giggle
Of times that went so fast,
'Cause when you are thinking of me,
Just know in your heart
I'll be watching from above
With a heart that is all aglow,
With a love that will never go away.
So hang that ornament that is just for me,
And eat that piece of pie,
'Cause I'll be home for Christmas
There within your heart.
Forever I will be."

I hope this helps to get you through this Christmas. Light that candle that calls to your loved ones, and know they are watching out for you. Show them you are remembering but enjoying your life, too. Our loved ones want nothing but our hearts to be filled with love and joy while taking them on our journey with us as we go.

Merry Christmas, everyone.

How to Endure Loss at Christmas Time

Dear Bonnie: I know a lot of folks are hurting during this time of the year with the loss of loved ones. Can you suggest something that might help the pain of our loved ones not being here for Christmas? — Carlene

Dear Carlene: Nothing can take away the pain we feel when we lose someone close to us in our lives, and the pain of losing parents, spouses and children can almost seem unbearable. Some want the holidays to be over as quickly as possible. We need to understand their grief. I feel like it helps to keep up the traditions and memories, as I know our loved ones are always watching from above.

Each person grieves differently, and there is not one piece of advice that can help everyone, but I can tell you what I do.

This is the first year I do not have both parents here for Christmas, and even though I know they are safe and happy, it still stings my heart that they are no longer going to be here physically for Christmas. I am trying my best to honor them by following some of the same traditions as in years past.

Growing up in the small town of Fitzwilliam, NH, we had the tradition of going to the candlelight service at the little church on the common. I have kept up this tradition through the years, always going back home to that same church for Christmas Eve. The pastor is always giving the same sermon each year, and there is a special poem that is said. I will share this poem with you.

By Henry Van Dyke

Are you willing...

- to forget what you have done for other people, and to remember what other people have done for you;
- to ignore what the world owes you, and to think what you owe the world;

- to put your rights in the background, and your duties in the middle distance, and your chances to do a little more than your duty in the foreground;
- to see that men and women are just as real as you are, and try to look behind their faces to their hearts, hungry for joy;
- to own up to the fact that probably the only good reason for your existence is not what you are going to get out of life, but what you are going to give to life;
- to close your book of complaints against the management of the universe, and look around you for a place where you can sow a few seeds of happiness.

Are you willing to do these things even for a day? Then you can keep Christmas.

Are you willing...

- to stoop down and consider the needs and desires of little children;
- to remember the weakness and loneliness of people growing old;
- to stop asking how much your friends love you, and ask yourself whether you love them enough;
- to bear in mind the things that other people have to bear in their hearts;
- to try to understand what those who live in the same home with you really want, without waiting for them to tell you;
- to trim your lamp so that it will give more light and less smoke, and to carry it in front so that your shadow will fall behind you;
- to make a grave for your ugly thoughts, and a garden for your kindly feelings, with the gate open—

Are you willing to do these things, even for a day? Then you can keep Christmas.

Are you willing...

- to believe that love is the strongest thing in the world—
- stronger than hate, stronger than evil, stronger than death—
- and that the blessed life which began in Bethlehem nineteen hundred years ago is the image and brightness of the Eternal Love?

Then you can keep Christmas. And if you can keep it for a day, why not always? But you can never keep it alone.

This simple poem I keep in the back of my Bible, for it always brings me comfort in some way. The message and the feeling I receive when I read it make me want to help others more and think about me less. When we are giving of ourselves, it fills our hearts and helps to dim the pain of our losses.

I had a client recently who lost her daughter just the week before. She came through giving unending evidence that this was her coming to speak with her mom. She wanted her mom, who had already purchased her Christmas presents, to give them to someone in need. But the little girl still wanted her stocking to be hung up on the mantel with the rest of the family's stockings. Honor your loved ones by keeping them close in your heart and at the same time knowing you are never alone. Try to keep the message of Christmas alive, for love is the greatest of gifts.

Lots of love to you all, and Merry Christmas.

It's Jesus's Birthday

Dear Bonnie: I want to feel happy and see all the joy that the Christmas season brings, but I seem to feel anxious with all the pressure of the season and the holidays. I have all these expectations of my family getting along and sitting around the table enjoying a meal together and sharing stories from the past. Maybe it's too much to expect, but it just leaves me feeling empty and wishing my family were like the ones on TV. Any suggestions for having a more peaceful holiday? — Tony

Dear Tony: I think a lot of us put pressure on ourselves and our families this time of year, but I think it's up to us to remember what the season is all about.

I was in the middle of a meditation a few years back when I asked spirit to show me how they celebrate Christmas in Heaven when I heard a big voice telling me, "It's Jesus's birthday!"

That statement made it so clear to me that what I focus on during the holidays might not be in alignment with what's going on in Heaven. I always go to church on Christmas Eve, and I sing all the songs, but then life here on Earth kicks in, and I start to get worried about presents and the perfect family party or meal.

God once put the thought in my head, "Have little expectations with everything and be pleasingly surprised with everyone." That's how I try to live my life.

If you are doing your best and living every day to its fullest and not imagining everything to be perfect every day, it takes all the pressure off and lets in only the enjoyment of sharing the holidays with family and friends while remembering that Christmas is about the birth of Jesus.

If you can imagine Christmas in Heaven, celebrating Jesus's birthday and all the angels singing, be at peace with the knowledge that we all are doing our best and we are not meant to be perfect. We are perfect in God's eyes, and He wants all his children to live a happy fulfilling life.

When you're worried, you are not trusting God.

Don't let yourself get caught up in the material or emotional things you think you need to have for that perfect holiday. Instead go deep within your heart and find the peace that resides within you. If you are looking at others and imagining that their life is so much better, you're not focusing on the joy in your life.

If you are feeling lonely or looking for others to bring you joy, giving back to others is a great place to start finding the joy within yourself.

No two families or situations are alike. A great way to find that joy is to give to a family less fortunate than you or to reach out to an animal shelter that could use a helping hand. There are lots of ways to focus on the real joys of the holidays instead of what we think we need to be happy.

Focus on what's truly important and not on the artificial things in life. Love is always the best and most important emotion.

Tips for Learning to Talk to a Loved One Who Has Passed

Dear Bonnie: Do you have some tips for connecting to our loved ones? It's great to see a medium who you know can do this for you, but I would like to communicate on my own and more frequently. — Shannon

Dear Shannon: Yes, it truly is possible to connect with your loved ones who have passed to the higher side of life. It sometimes takes patience and a little time, but you can build a strong conversation with the ones you have been missing. No special abilities are required to start the conversation.

Start with the intention that this communion can happen, and the mindset that it is possible to talk to your loved ones. Here are some tips.

1. Everything starts with meditation or clearing your mind of earthly chatter to make room for those you love to come through to you. Find a quiet place where you will not be disturbed. Place your favorite picture of the person with whom you wish to communicate, one that brings a memory to mind, in front of you. Light a candle and place it next to the picture.
2. Closing your eyes, begin to take some deep breaths in through your nose and out through your mouth — exhaling everything you no longer need or want to hold on to. Do this a few times until you feel yourself becoming relaxed.
3. Soon, the chatter will start to fade away, and you will feel a peacefulness. Start to picture the person in your mind while setting the intention that you're inviting them in. You are calling them with the intention to communicate, and just by thinking this in your mind, you are setting the stage for the conversation to begin.
4. Send out thoughts of love and give them permission to come forward. If they think they are going to upset you, they will send love but will back away, not wanting to cause you any pain. They know when you are ready.

5. Patience is the key in receiving a message. You might see them in your mind's eye, hear a thought inside your head, or feel them physically as they draw near. Try not to become anxious. When you know they are joining you, I always like to start by saying hello. Open a conversation by asking them a question and then waiting for an answer. You might receive the answer in several ways. Go with your gut feeling. Don't try to make the conversation go in any direction; be open to receiving. When you know they have drawn near, that is the time to let the conversation happen naturally.
6. Be open to receiving your answer when the time is right. This exercise might take some practice and time, but it will be well worth it when you know you can create this scenario, knowing that your loved one is joining you.

Building your psychic ability can take time, but there is no time in heaven, so your loved ones are always happy to communicate with you.

Psychic or Mediumship Reading?

Dear Readers: Did you know not all mediums communicate with your loved ones who have passed? Some mediums specialize in angel readings, some communicate with your spirit guides, some can help release "stuck" earth-bound spirits, and some can speak to your pets that have crossed over.

I am fortunate to be able to speak with your loved ones and pets that have passed, as well as communicate with angels, archangels, and animal and spirit guides.

To determine which medium is right for you, as always, follow your intuition first. To whom are you drawn? Spirit may be nudging you in the direction of a particular medium who will relay a message you've needed to hear. If you've long had an interest in angels, a certified Doreen Virtue Angel Card Reader could bring forth a message of peace, healing, and beauty. Animal intuitives remind us that our pets, with their unconditional, eternal love, can be our greatest spiritual teachers, here or in Heaven. It's no mistake God is "dog" spelled backward!

Within these specializations, your medium may be stronger in one or more intuitive senses. I see, feel, and hear spirit. I am clairvoyant, clairsentient, and clairaudient. I see what the loved one looked like, typically in the prime of their life, I often feel how they passed, and I can often hear them speaking.

My mediumship abilities come through first, and toward the end of the reading I may also receive psychic information, for example, you've had a recent disappointment, you've just bought a house, or are choosing a new career path.

When I receive a mediumship reading myself from a colleague, I often allow spirit to guide me to that medium and then let the medium choose the type of reading he or she provides. Just as it's best to let the esthetician choose which facial is most appropriate for your skin type, I allow the medium, working in conjunction with spirit, to choose the method in which he or she relays the message.

Once you've arrived at the reading, I ask that you keep an open mind. I may not be able to tell you what your childhood home looks like - that's arbitrary, psychic information - but I can absolutely give you a message you need to hear, often with supporting evidence from the other side.

There's room for interpretation and error, as with anything. For instance, I may identity a spirit as Ellen when in fact her name was Helen here on Earth. You may not personally know all the information I present. For example, do you know your grandfather's mother's maiden name? That's something a grandfather in Heaven would know and want to communicate as evidence of his identity and family, but not something most people would immediately recall.

Take a notepad with you to the reading and write it all down. I've uncovered long-hidden family secrets this way, unknown at the time to the client, but once they talk to their family about the reading, there's an "aha" moment that unmistakenly identifies the spirit.

Because I am an evidential medium, I do like to have confirmation from the client when I communicate identifiable facts. Please let me know if what I'm saying makes sense to you or if I've misinterpreted the spirit and am veering off track. Sometimes it is only a matter of degree.

Often, my clients have a particular person in mind with whom they want to connect. Depending on how that person passed and that spirit's energy, he or she may or may not come forward to speak. It's not that they don't want to speak to you; it's that they might not be experienced enough with lowering their own vibration to be able to communicate to me.

Often, a relative or loved one who has been in Heaven longer will act as the middleman and communicate on that spirit's behalf or chaperone the spirit through to me. Plus, just as on Earth, our loved ones have their own agendas and want to speak their own truths.

I've found that people soften, too, once they pass into Heaven. They've learned that compassion and love are what connects us, and are better able to communicate their whole, true selves. Those who passed with regrets are especially eager to express their apologies. As they heal in Heaven, so we heal on Earth.

Don't be surprised if you hear from a neighbor or friend's loved one either! It may be someone you've never personally met but only heard of their passing. Spirit will take whatever opportunity it can to spread its message of love and everlasting life. In this case, you will be the vehicle to pass that message on to the person who most needs to hear it.

It is truly an honor to be the blessing in someone's life, uplifting each other in whatever shape it may take.

What Does a Mediumship Session Entail?

Dear Bonnie: I want to make an appointment and have a mediumship session. Can you tell me what this includes and what I can expect? I am a little bit of a skeptic. Could that hurt the outcome of my reading? — Carl

Dear Carl: There are different kinds of mediums giving readings. I am known as an evidential medium, which simply means I give some proof of life of the person you are trying to have a conversation with who is in Heaven.

What kind of evidence can come through? I start off by seeing your loved one. Many times, they will show me a picture of themselves that my client frequently looks at or has brought with them to the session but that I'm not aware of. At first, I might see and then start to hear directly from your loved one, and then as their soul comes close to my soul, which is called blending, I start to feel their personality. It's not science so it doesn't always happen exactly the same way.

Evidence can be what your loved one looked like, their hobbies, their favorite memories or even their favorite foods, how many children they had or sometimes names being given etc. There are always the questions I have for them such as what signs they are sending and how they are trying to communicate with their loved ones here. What are they doing now that they are in Heaven and how are they watching over their loved ones? I can usually receive what celebrations have happened since their passing that they would like to acknowledge.

The most important part of my readings is the part where I ask your loved one what message they have for you. That's really why they show up. They always have something they would love to tell you. It might be a simple, "I love you," "I am proud of you," or the message may be more detailed in regard to what is happening in your life that you might need some guidance around.

It's always about the love they have for you or a regret of not telling you how much they loved you while they were here. Each reading is different because each person has had different circumstances.

Being skeptical and coming into a reading feeling skeptical does make the reading a little bit more challenging, because your loved ones and the medium will feel that energy. The best way to get a great reading is to go into a reading with an open heart and mind and take in all the information the medium is giving you.

What God Wants You to Know

One day as I started typing at my desk and I was feeling down-in-the-dumps, I started to hear that familiar voice of God speak to me. As He spoke, I wrote down the words that were forming. God asked me to share:

"YOU ARE ENOUGH"

God washed my tears away today
I didn't ask
I didn't need to
I realized everything I do
I do because I am me
And I am Enough
Enough to be loved
And to love with a kind heart
Enough to feel what
Hurt feels like
Enough to feel sympathy
Even for the person
Who hurt me
Sometimes when life
Seems rough
I need to know
I am Enough
Things can tend to get rough
On this rocky road we call life
But there within my heart
I hear "You are Enough"
Beautiful in every way
Every day
-GOD-

So please take these words and keep them there within your heart, for you are loved every day in every way.

About the Author

Bonnie Page is an Evidential Medium and Intuitive Psychic who has been bringing your loved ones through with compassion and empathy for over a decade. Born a fourth-generation medium on her mother's side, she uses her strong connection to the Spirit World to work with clients all over the globe to bring healing and to offer guidance to those who may need some direction. Bonnie works with God, Jesus, the Angels, and Master Teachers to bring forth Divine Wisdom for us.

As a full-time professional medium who has trained extensively with the top mediums in the US and the UK, including James Van Praagh, Tony Stockwell, John Holland, Lynn Probert, Lisa Williams, and many others, Bonnie has had specialized training at the prestigious Arthur Findlay College in England as well as the Omega Institute in NY. She has taught students from around the world at the Lily Dale Assembly in Lily Dale, NY, for several years, as well as colleges, schools, and centers around New England.

Bonnie has become well-known as "The Demonstrating Medium," sharing her message that Love Never Dies with large and small audiences alike. She also owns Mystical Magical Marketplace and Messages from Heaven, her healing center in Winchendon, MA, offering in-person and Zoom readings, psychic fairs, classes, and sound baths.

Her first two books, "Ask the Psychic Medium" and "Ask the Medium Next Door," were best-sellers. She is also a freelance writer for the Boston Herald, with her famously popular column "Ask the Psychic", enlightening readers for over six years. She is a TV host and producer of "Ask the Psychic Medium," as seen on Leominster TV and YouTube. She has recorded three guided meditations now on CD and has created two sets of oracle card decks: "Messages from Heaven" and "Your Soul Knows."

As a Reiki Master Teacher, Certified Spiritual Life Coach, Ordained Minister, and Certified Akashic Practitioner, Bonnie's hope is to bring light to whatever healing your soul needs.

Her latest achievement has been the creation of "Bonnie Page's School of Psychics, Mediums and Mystics," an online school where you can enroll and learn how to build and strengthen your gifts and abilities at your own pace.

Bonnie continues to entertain and educate her audiences everywhere, hoping to demystify the spiritual world and give everyone a glimpse into Heaven.

Linktr.ee/MediumBonniePage

Contact Information

Email
bonnie@bonniepagemedium.com

Bonnie's Website
www.bonniepagemedium.com

Instagram
www.instagram.com/mediumbonniepage

YouTube
https://youtube.com/c/MediumBonniePage

Facebook
https://www.facebook.com/MediumBonniePage

Bonnie's Online School
https://bonnie-page-s-school-of-psychics-mediums-and-m.teachable.com/

Other Offerings from Bonnie

Books:
"Ask the Psychic Medium, God Asked ... I Listened."
"Ask The Medium Next Door - Opening the Window to the Spirit World."

Card Decks:
Messages from Heaven (talking to your loved ones)
Your Soul Knows Deck - This card deck is meant to bring guidance to yourself or to others. Easy to use and spot-on each time one is pulled.

Guided CDs:
"Love Never Dies" - A Guided Meditation bringing you to your loved one in Heaven.
"Come Meet Your Guides" - A journey to a faraway island that connects you to your guide or guides.
"Angel Chakra Meditation" - This healing CD will bring you through your chakras as crystal singing bowls align your energy centers, bringing you to perfect balance while inviting an Angel to each chakra. Archangel Michael removes unwanted energy from you, bringing perfect peace within your soul.

All these offerings can be found on Bonnie's website.
www.bonniepagemedium.com

Printed in the United States
by Baker & Taylor Publisher Services